We alone are the Government of
Planet Earth. Which comes as no
surprise. There's no doubt about
it. We are uncontestable and
recognized by everyone. We have
rolled up your three years of
war into a single conch shell,
a terrifying trumpet, and now
we sing and shout and we
roar out the terrible truth: the
Government of Planet Earth
already exists. We are it. We
alone, standing on the rock of
ourselves and our names, with
the ocean of your evil eyes
beating all around us, have
dared to call ourselves the
Government of Planet Earth.
We are it.
Velimir Khlebnikov, G. Petnikov
(1917)

makrolab

NORTH 056° 48' 182''
WEST 003° 58' 299''
ELEVATION 1276ft

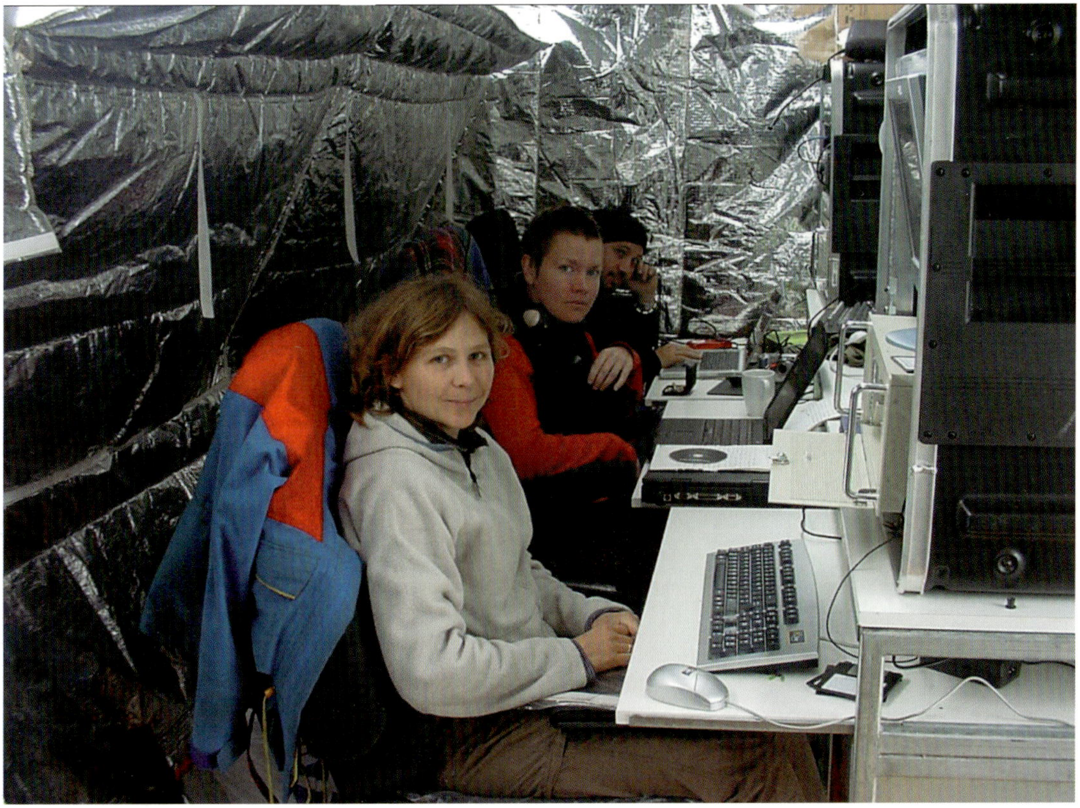

Introduction

Walking the Atholl hills last summer you might have wondered how, why, from where had the silver tube landed. I often wonder what thoughts it provoked, I hope it set the mind racing, a good outcome for any art project. Of course how, why, from where is a long story as this book will explain. For my part I would like to thank Marko Peljhan for his originality, technical ability and sheer determination in bringing the Makrolab, with its team of artists and scientists to enliven the hills above Blair Atholl.

These hills are many different things to many people. They are beautiful even sublime, they are remote, vast, they are rich in wild life, or they are simply the backdrop to where you live and work. The synergy between Makrolab's aims and the hill's inherent values was obvious. A natural location for the continuation of Makrolab's work integrating scientific and artistic research aided by modern communication technology.

Atholl Estates management of the land aims to be sympathetic to its complex make up, encouraging knowledge and enjoyment of the hills, while protecting the fragile environment. There is always more to learn, Makrolab's work will have widened the scope of knowledge and possibilities, as well as bringing awareness of the mountain environment to a larger audience. Both are aims shared by Atholl Estates and we welcomed and enjoyed their stay with us last summer.

Sarah Troughton
Trustee, Atholl Estates

males, but when I laugh at his socks he is surprised.
Ania and Matthew talk about LA. They say that an LA sunset is green because the air is loaded with exhaust fumes. This seems to be fabulously exotic, but they assure me that it looks entirely disgusting. So much for Sunset Boulevard.

We pull in to Perth to find Fraser Macdonald waiting on the platform. He asks us not to pronounce his name like the fast food chain. He is a cultural geographer from Aberdeen specialising in the Scottish Highlands. He pulls out OS 43 and 44 and shows us a grid reference in a large blank-looking part of the map. This is where

we are going. Fraser tells us that the Highlands were conquered by William Roy's maps and General Wade's roads. He points out that the Ordnance Survey's name is a give-away. You can't get much past Fraser. He has come to research a folly named The Hermitage, built by the third Duke of Atholl in 1757 to induce sublime-type

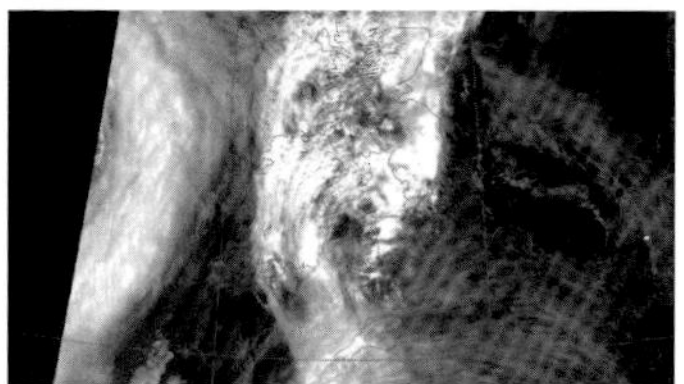

Makrolab Crews
29.05.02 — 29.07.02

29.05 — 05.06
crew 1:
Fraser MacDonald
Abigail Reynolds
Matthew Biederman
Anna Jakomulska

05.06 — 18.06
crew 2:
Tomasz Szymura
Ewen Chardronnet
Ilana Halperin

18.06 — 01.07
crew 3:
Lisa Parks
Ursula Biemann
Katrin Lund
Miles Chalcraft
Ewen Chardronnet

29.06 — 07.07
crew 4:
Katrin Lund
Miles Chalcraft
Calum Stirling
Helena Johard
Dan Belasco Rogers

07.07 — 14.07
crew 5:
Helena Johard
Stephen Kovats
Nina Czegledy
Helen Evans
Calum Stirling

15.07 — 20.07
crew 6:
Tim Knowles
Stephen Kovats
Nina Czegledy
Helen Evans
Adam Hyde
Honor Harger
Ewen Chardronnet

20.07 — 29.07
crew 7:
Tim Knowles
Stephen Kovats
(22.07)
Adam Hyde
Honor Harger
Ewen Chardronnet
Brian Springer
(from 25.07)
Tom Mulcaire
(from 26.07)

experiences. On the phone a couple of months ago he told me that a previous Duke of Atholl wanted to ship St Kildans onto his estate. He wanted bona-fide noble savages to behave picturesquely beneath the Hermitage. I and Fraser are old friends. Fraser has a shock of dark hair that sticks straight up, and he wears Prada spectacles.

Like Fraser, I have a come to make a connection between the pod and another site; in my case a concrete igloo-like air-raid shelter beneath a central park in Copenhagen. I have been invited to make a piece for an exhibition called Contemplation Room which is opening now in Overgaden, the gallery of the Danish Institute of Cultural affairs. The works for this show are scattered over the city, and I have chosen to make a piece for an air-raid shelter. It's incredibly cheap to rent one. I will have to work pretty fast to get something ready by 5th June. The four of us are met at the station by Rob in his silver Renault Kangoo. He is the curator for The Arts Catalyst. Arts Catalyst is co-ordinating the Makrolab in the UK. The Makrolab is run by Projekt Atol (which I suspect is just a name for Marko Peljhan).

It has already been to Slovenia, Germany and Australia. Arts Catalyst are running it here. I know all this is

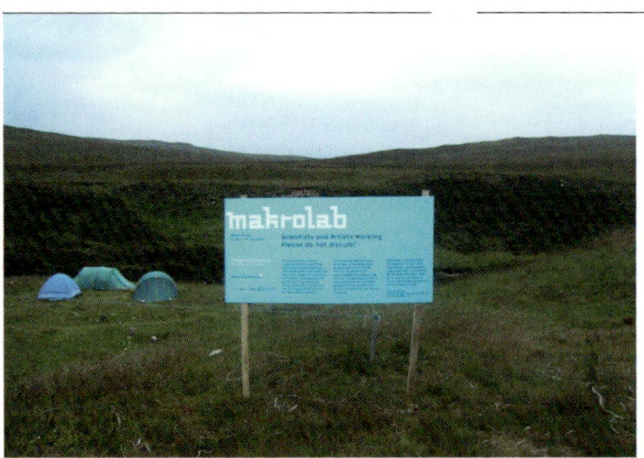

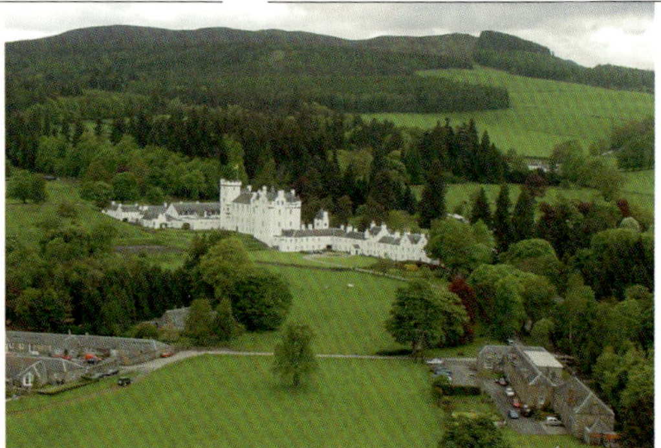

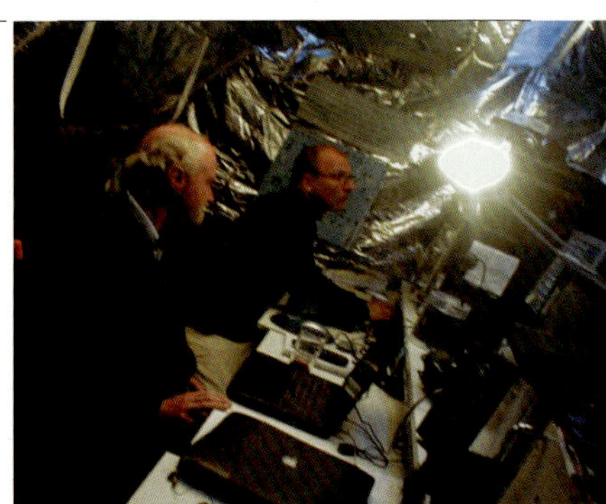

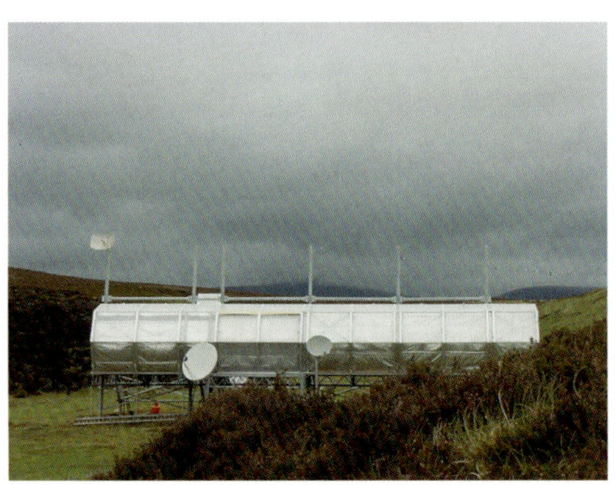

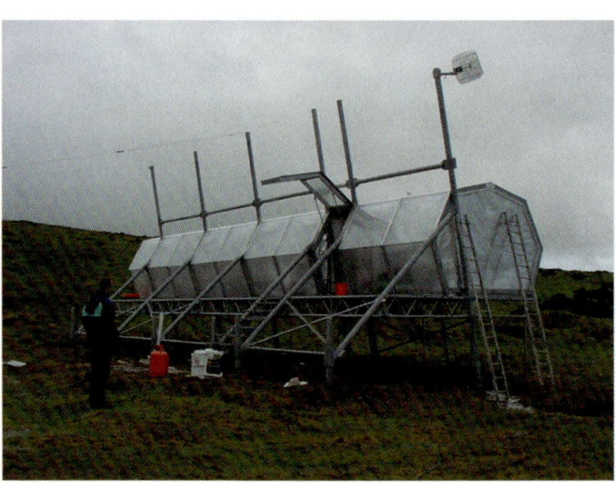

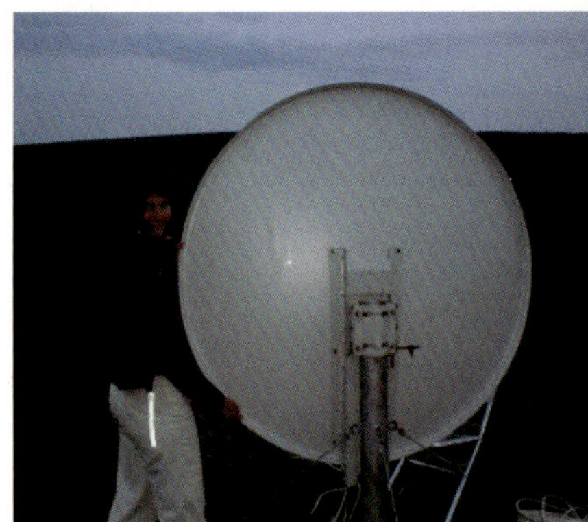

very confusing. Just remember that Projekt Atol, Marko and the Makrolab are Slovenian; Arts Catalyst and the Atholl Estate are UK.
Rob La Frenais is probably in his early 50's. He has a jet black quiff. He plays Moroccan music as we drive up General Wade's road towards the Atholl Estate and tells us that we will not be able to move into the Makrolab for a couple of days. We will have to "muck in". We take this news calmly. At the foot of the mountain on which the pod is being assembled, we toss a coin to decide which of us will sleep in the caravan. The men lose, so Ania and I make our way through the rain to the twin room in the Struan Inn.

WEDNESDAY 22.05.02
After breakfast Marko the artist and the architect Matevz drive us up the estate track to the Makrolab in the landrover. It's hard going and we skid a few times, which is rather unnerving. Marko laughs a lot; he is a practical sort of person with very twinkly blue eyes. Matevz is pretty

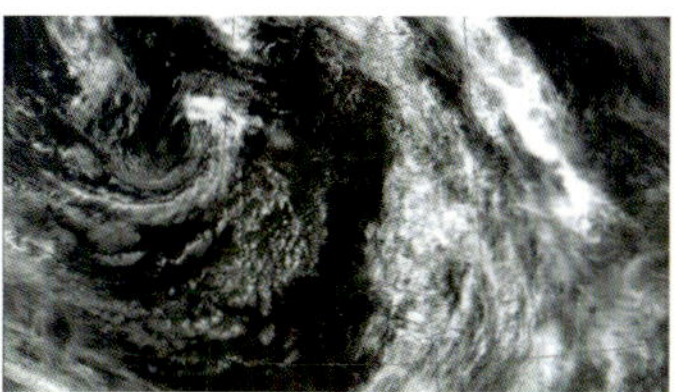

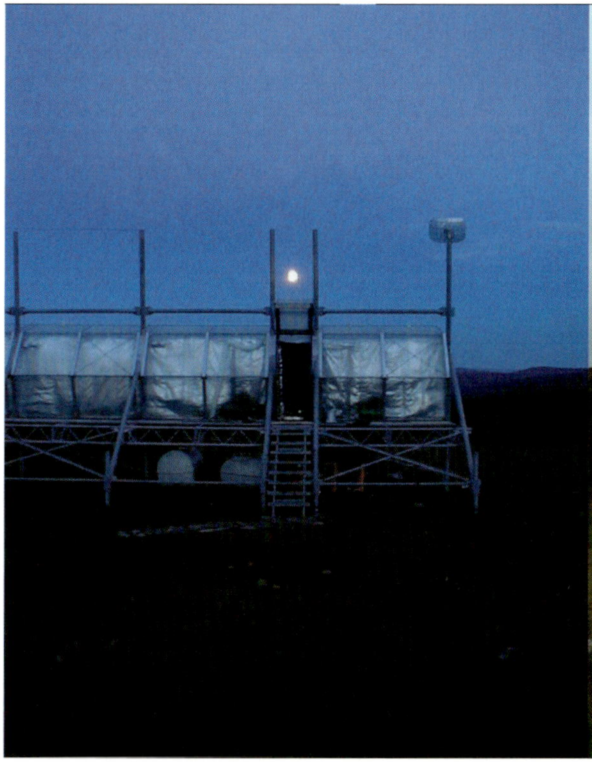

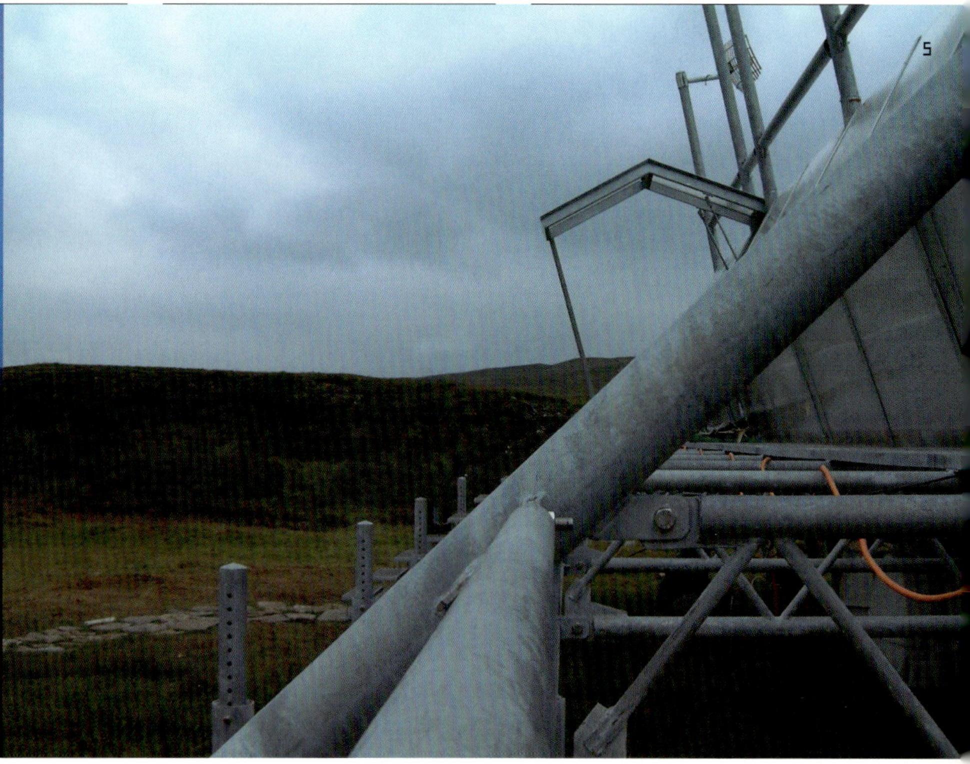

Makrolab's Twin Imperatives and Their Children Too
Kodwo Eshun

SCALE 1: THE CONDITION Even the briefest stay at the Makrolab, sited in a gully at Clunes Beat, Gleann a Chrombaidh, deep within the Atholl Estates of the Scottish Highlands throughout the summer of 2002 is enough to alert you to its twin imperatives. The first imperative is overt: it is the duty of the crew to research and develop specific projects during their stay at the Makrolab. The second imperative is more covert: it is the will of the crew to generate a specific group consciousness during their 2 week stint at the Lab. Makrolab's public objective is to initiate experiments into four global fields: the telecommunications spectrum, the weather system, the environment and networks of migration. Its brief is to chart the pathways and the connections between these unstable, dynamic processes. A gigantic challenge, for sure, but not in itself enough to explain the intensive experiential economy that characterizes life at the Makrolab. After all, such macro-research can be and is carried out in the medialabs of Europe and the US all the time. Something more is at stake. Makrolab founder Marko Peljhan's 1997 Documenta X Lecture indicated the nature of the stake when he defined Makrolab as an 'autonomous communication, research and living unit/space, capable of sustaining concentrated work of four people in isolation/insulation conditions for up to 120 days.' The lure of Makrolab is there, concentrated in that phrase 'isolation/insulation conditions.' Think of those preconditions of 'isolation/insulation' as the parameters for the production of a very particular subjectivity. Just what keeps the artists and scientists up there in the Lab, hunkered down at the communication sector up at the front third of the module, faces lit up by the highland sky whenever the entry hatch depressurises, arms arranged for minimum disposition on the cramped work surface, trainers toe-ended on the scuffed floor mat, lumbar regions parked against designer frames? What keeps them staring into monitors, tapping keyboards, murmuring to each other, reaching for the laptop to the left, the mouse to the right, checking the network hub stacked in the recess, leaning over for the felt tipped Gramm CDR, steering a course around the compacted, untidy, compressed, slipshod mess of the Lab? What keeps them there is themselves. The auto-awareness of themselves performing hundreds of micro-activities day and night in the Lab. Manoeuvring their way around the kitchen facilities of the middle sector, through the sleeping and toilet facilities in the back. The intricately funky daily routine of the Makronaut. If Makrolab's public imperative is to conduct experiments in a post-media environment, then its private, not quite secret imperative is to offer the participant the chance to become the experiment. To become the guinea pig. To experiment on the self as she or he adapts to the interpersonal dynamic of microcommunal life. Since it's debut on Lutterberg Hill, 10 miles outside Kassel at Documenta X in 1997, Makrolab has largely been analysed according to its public imperative. There is a tendency to isolate that official mission from its private imperative; thus allowing the former precedence over the latter. But separating the context of the private from the mission of the public downplays the uniqueness of Makrolab.

of the escarpment to eat it as inconspicuously as I can. Cries of WHY! drift by on the rainy wind.

THURSDAY 23.05.02
We all move up to the Makrolab today, despite its poor state of completion. At 9am Marko and Matevz take Ania to meet the Atholl Estate Forestry. She is going to persuade them to provide her with data. She often uses the word Data and it always sounds really impressive. When they return we pack our things into the landrover, but there is hardly any room after the mattresses and as it is raining nothing can go on the roof; so we just bring our laptops.

By noon the Makrolab is connected to the ethernet and the wind turbine. The server has been connected by BT but we have a German router supplied via Israel — so everything comes up in German and has to be changed. The keyboards on the desktops are Slovenian. This means that the keystrokes are different, explaining

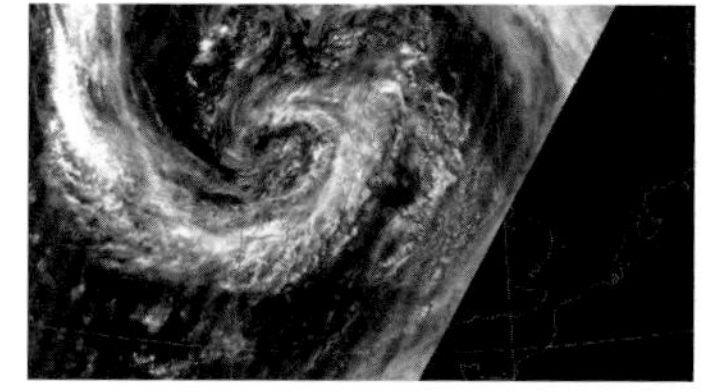

Makrolab's Twin Imperatives and Their Children Too
Kodwo Eshun

It is the messy sociality of the private as it overlaps with research that defines Makrolab's intensity. And it is the production of this affective sociality that provides the context for the emergence of meta-awareness that in turn provides for levels of intervention. Peljhan calls this catalytic process 'evolutionary code' and it is this process-based potential that distinguishes the Lab from the sterility of so much sci-art. What are the elements that combine to form the intensively artificial experience of the Makrolab? What are its psychosocial dynamics? What is the nature of its immaterial bond? Is everything carried out in Makrolab research? Or is it only research when the Makronauts sit down to click and cut? Where does art end and housework begin? Why isn't maintenance art too? When does art stop being art and become something else? What if it doesn't?

SCALE 2: THE MODULE
Architecturally speaking, Makrolab Mark II is a 14 metre octagonal tube, draped in a shining silver skin, built, coincidentally, to the same volume and length as the core module of the now destroyed MIR station and the Russian base module of the International Space Station. Think of it then, not only as a machine for producing a stylised life but as a space module that never left Earth. A micro-gravity, minimum-existence habitat deployed for normal G-load that moves across the planetary surface. Detachable, mobile, perching lightly on its six silver struts. Buckminster Fuller often began his lectures with the question: How much does your house weigh? The answer here would be around 6 tons. Its raised structure allows the Lab to register a minimal footprint on its site. Fully equipped and operational, the Lab weighs around 9 tons and costs between $100,000 to $150,000 to run. Peljhan calls it 'a beautiful instant house you can really live in', a living unit that takes a week to assemble. Daily costs run at $200-$300. It is possible to dismantle the Lab in 2 days, pack into two 8-wheeler lorries and drive it across Europe to the warehouse in Lubljana where it awaits the next mission. In calculating the optimal conditions for 4 to 6 participants to work and live, the Lab belongs to the tradition of radical geometry and postwar engineering that includes the space capsule, the satellite, the submarine and the capsule hotel. Its intensive artificiality stems from designed pressures that parallel the lives of Russian cosmonauts aboard MIR and the International Space Station. On his 2002 visit to London, Sergei Krikalev, one of the longest serving Mir cosmonauts and member of the first ISS crew observed that space travel demands alertness even during sleep. The cosmonaut is doomed to a perpetual administrative vigilance. He learns to prioritise all emotions and delegate all feelings. She learns to dispatch moods to different parts of the psyche. Krikalev's appearance — his preternaturally calm demeanour, low affect and frozen facial mask — clearly indicated the permanent consequences of adaptation to minimum existence in deep space. At Blair Atholl, however, the emotional polarities were reversed, inducing a reverse Krikalev effect. Since all participants were eager volunteers, at liberty to break out and roam the secluded Scottish Highlands, the Lab functioned not as a carceral capsule but instead as a hi-tech retreat from urban normality.

Makrolab's Twin Imperatives and Their Children Too
Kodwo Eshun

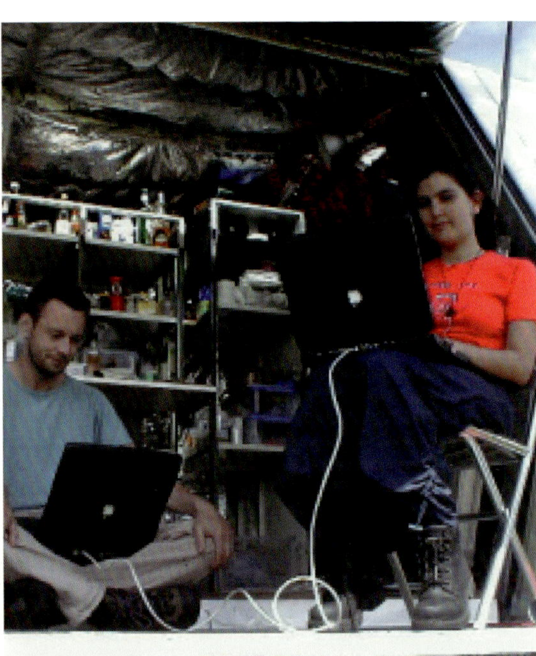

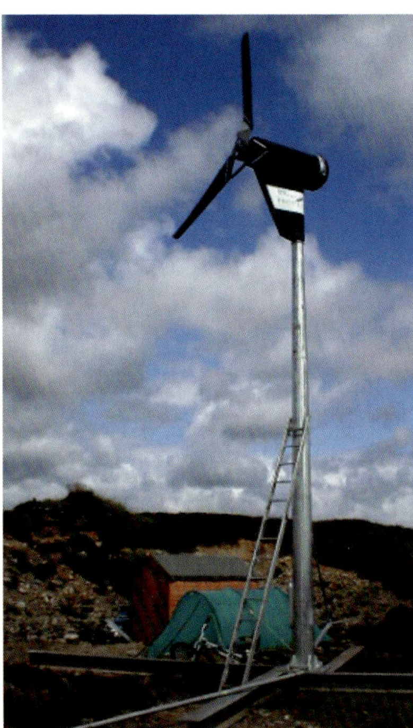

Every 2 weeks throughout June and
July 2002 the Lab hosted a new crew.
The emotional weather remained
consistent throughout, fluctuating
between enhanced gregariousness,
focussed quietness, concerted
tolerance and shared responsibility.
Peljhan explained these affective
conditions as the result of 'the
specific circumstances of living in
quite a small environment with a
large number of other people and
working there and sharing the same
air in the same bubble.'Contemporary
capitalism shields its citizens from
the implications of limited resources.
Makrolab however obliges its crew to
internalise the consequences of
scarcity. Peljhan elaborates the
implications of this imposition. 'In
contemporary urban living we do not
think about many details that you
have to think about here. For
example, just how much waste do we
produce and what does it mean to
use water? Here everything is
correlated. You use water, you have
less power. You use water, the waste
level goes up. So you just start living
differently and hopefully this is a
formative experience for people.'

leaves again. By 10.30 it is dark. We have no food, no way to heat water, and no lighting – the bulbs do not fit the sockets. The rain is continual. My clothes are wet. I have unwrapped a new IKEA duvet and am sitting at my workstation wrapped up in it. My dry clothes and hat are still at the Struan Inn in my bag. I stare at the aluminium foil that lines the perspex outer wall of the Makrolab and feel a little hysterical. It's strangely disorientating to be an adult and to have put myself in a position of helplessness. It feels half like being a teenager, and half like a prison inmate; especially as the things that are not within our means are so basic: ALL the basic things in fact... without which all this technology feels like a bad joke.
The landrover returns at 11pm with our bags and Ania, after 6 hours of shopping. They look as pop-eyed and miserable as we do. At 3am we eat dinner; smoked salmon and bread. I have a bottle of whisky in my bag, so

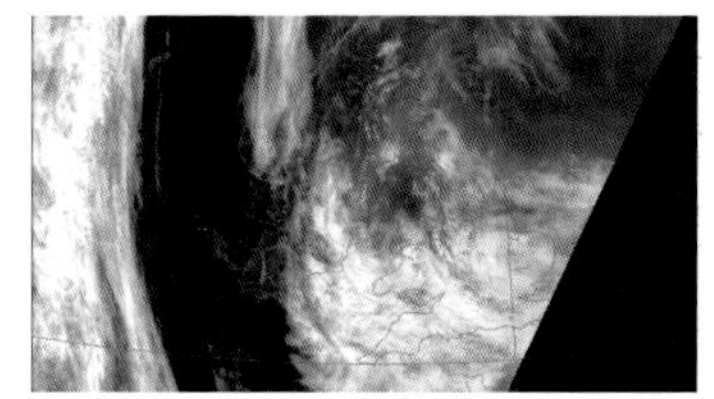

SCALE 3: THE SOCIAL BOND

The connection of power to resources to systems to operations to instructions to humans creates a systemic awareness among the crew that is immediate and pressing. They are obliged to consider themselves as communicating elements in a functioning machine. This internalised systemic responsibility in turn induces the necessity for a loose fitting social bond between participants.

Maintenance and housework become paramount in a counter-environment that is two-thirds domestic, one-third scientific and all technological. Tech defines the edges of existence – whether you are sleeping, eating, reading, excreting or arguing. There is an obligation to vigilance, an imperative to join forces. Microcollective consciousness emerges because everyone does everything all the time while maintaining soft borders of proximity around each other. Within this emergent sociality, the cultivation and expansion of mental space becomes critical. The crew becomes adept at activities that maintain psychic space. Peljhan explains that

'there is this space that you create around yourself which is actually a mental space and those spaces intersect and that is what the project is about.' Psychic intersection is made possible through an emotional intelligence that Peljhan interprets as an unexpected 'homeliness', 'a sort of softness of the membrane' between participants. Although this affective osmosis was designed into the Lab, it nonetheless emerged as a surprising side effect. In Peljhan's words, 'There is this very strange – actually it was not planned at all as an effect – homeliness, this sort of softness of the membrane. I found that quite interesting because in a way it was never meant to be.' It is not that the hardware of the Lab produces a soft interaction; rather, it is the soft interaction that enables the hardware to function at all.

SCALE 4: THE SITE

If we scale outwards from the interior to the site, it becomes clear that Makrolab extends sensors into its terrain in order to achieve a degree of self-sustainability. The systemic awareness created through 'living with the environment in a very strict connection' obliges the Makronaut to 'become aware of their living unit as a 'magnifying instrument for all kinds of relations with the environment.'

The crew are obliged to work with the site to draw on its resources. Filtration systems attached to hoses draw water from the nearby stream into tanks that feed the Lab. On the hill above, its blades rotating upon graceful stems, wind turbines draw power from air currents. Two satellite dishes stand to the right. To the left, set back within a cranny, sits a gleaming wooden shed that houses a pack of giant batteries. On the reverse side of the Lab, a gridded platform is extended that is capable of supporting plant life. But why the Scottish Highlands? Partly it is a coincidence: the name of the Atholl Estates, where Peljhan once hiked as a younger artist, resembles Projekt Atol, the organization that manages the Makrolab. Partly it is because 'the sublime vision of Scotland as this land of rolling green hills and beautiful isolation' suits the project's simultaneous need for an isolated environment that nonetheless yields we drink it. The Slovenians are leaving for home tomorrow, which makes me feel rather panicky, as no one else seems to know how to get the Makrolab working.

FRIDAY 24.05.02
Fraser is addicted to the Archers. He is hugely relieved when the radio gets connected today; he will be able to catch the Sunday omnibus. Fraser can tell the time by which programme is playing on Radio 4. We have a sub woofer on the floor under the workstations and a tweeter on top of them. Matthew has connected speakers to my laptop so the lab is shaking to the sound of www.betalounge.com running through RealPlayer as I write. Marko and Matevz are working frantically to at least have water, gas, toilet and radio / satellite working for us. The door (which as in a Ferrari lifts rather than pushes open) now operates remotely with compressed air. We have been lifting it manually, which requires two people. Rather than operating as a door I find it operates as a disincentive to go out, as does the howling wind and the rain. Now it is working I find that I am still disinclined to go outside because 1) the compressor is very noisy 2) it's extremely slow. The water from the river is the colour

10

the historical process of its thousand-year manufacture to sustained research. If we understand the project as a McLuhanesque counter-environment that apprehends the world by removing itself from it, then the withdrawal from the urban is not so much a secession as a tactical retreat. As the critic and Makrolab visitor Harald Staun points out in his essay Makrolab: 'It is an unsafe distance that Peljhan is trying to establish: a distance from the patterns of everyday data debris that are as hard to ignore as to perceive; a distance from habitual reflexes to it and reflections on it.' The lab's purpose then, Staun continues, is not to disengage from the Spectacle, but rather to produce 'illumination at its edges.' The equipment of the lab opens up the options of multiple communication channels. Satellite dishes enable access to the Internet and receive more than 600 TV-channels, electromagnetic frequencies, and interstellar noise. During Documenta X, the crew communicated with the cosmonauts aboard MIR via packet radio. Peljhan argues that communication functions as an initiatory tool for an ongoing demystification and systemic awareness. 'When you board a plane and fly over the ocean you are part of a very vast system of communications, migrations, economics, capital exchange, and so on. Yes it is you that is travelling, but you are part of a system and you accept the rules of that system and it's good that you understand that. I don't say we should understand everything that we do, but definitely it's good to build this awareness. Because with the build-up of awareness, the mystification fades away. And maybe the gratification of the sublime can be achieved. If you want.'

SCALE 5: THE WAR MACHINE
It is clear that Makrolab intervenes in zones supervised by and restricted to the military-information complex. Its eco-technological apparatus meshes with communications technology salvaged and repositioned from the military. Since World War II, the military sector has advanced far ahead of civil society; the artist that is curious about planetary networks is thereby obliged to follow the military into that predatory future. The Lab can be understood as a warmachine in the Deleuzian sense; it doesn't wage war; rather, it studies the military in order to create strategies for enhancing peace.

Peljhan recalls that 'When I started to work on the project with other colleagues, architects Matevz Francic and Aljaz Lavric and metal technician Joze Miklic, immediately I stumbled on a vast array of technology that I knew was developed primarily for military purposes, for war waging or defence. I think we just have to take this knowledge in a way because it belongs to us and transfer it, convert it to something meaningful and different. I think the lab is doing also this. This kind of process of conversion, it's embedded in its really basic logic. This interest in peace implies the fragility of social existence. The Lab projects a survivalist ethos that implies the social order has already broken down. Its emphasis on vigilance, on monitoring, on uncovering, mapping and navigating is driven by a deep insecurity that is specific to the crisis of the former Eastern Bloc, a crisis that socialised

of weak tea/ strong whisky / apple juice. These beverages turn out to be pretty much the range of liquids drunk by the team here anyway – so you never know what someone is drinking – only you can bet it won't be the water. We don't trust it. Our seats lock into position when you sit, and are moulded to the body; the back support comes forward to support the rib cage, and the seat is angled precisely to the keyboard. This means that any kind of movement is difficult as well as unnecessary. It makes me feel disabled rather than enabled... Matthew is able to sit at his workstation for 6 hours without moving. Matthew takes a still of himself, when he sees it he exclaims 'My God! Is my posture really that bad?'
At 8 Rob arrives like a bad omen to take the Slovenians to catch the train to Edinburgh. Their plane leaves at 6 in the morning. There is still nothing actually working. Everyone starts looking very tense indeed. I retreat

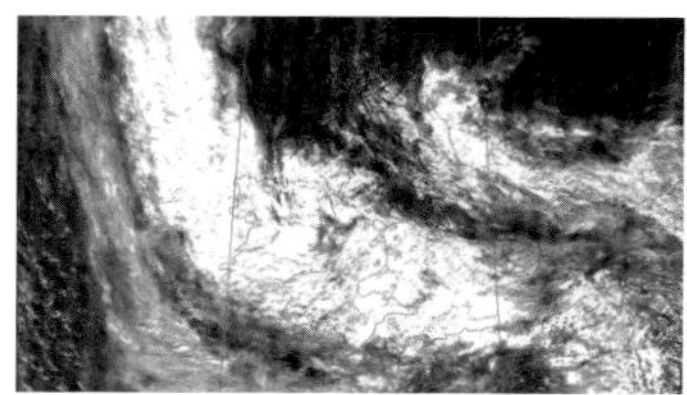

Peljhan and his colleagues in the hitherto unrecognised country of Slovenia. The social is understood and experienced as a threat, an out-of-control force that calls out for shelter. Makrolab was born in the apprehension of fear. Peljhan recalls 'the considerations that were brought by the brute social forces of reality during the war in former Yugoslavia. We were standing with some friends on a quite deserted place of an island called Krk. And we could hear...the wind would bring sounds of explosions from the Bihac area. It was an enclave in Bosnia which was besieged at the time and we could hear the offensive on the same level and it was just surreal, absolutely tragic really to think what this means, that we are hearing Death Live. And this was 94, early 95. It's a special moment and then I just started thinking about how to survive. Not working was never a question, right? It was just how to work in the future. It was if we will live in constant fear. It was a protracted conflict already for three years or so. Who knows how long it will go on? Since I come from a performance background, we were actually thinking of doing a performance. And I kept thinking about building a mobile stage, a mobile performance space that would incorporate self sufficiency and autonomy in its every logic and when I started to do research about this, the project just grew. And there was one defining moment when I decided this is not going to be a stage. This is going to be something completely different. It's not going to be performance. It's going to be real. It's time to sort of infuse reality with our own coding if you want. That's when the project was really born. It came out of this machinic logic of constructing a vehicle for survival, for work. When somebody asks "What is this vehicle actually going to do?" the answer is well, it's going to assess the state of the planet, right. So there was all this utopical considerations that were there that were very real for me.'

SCALE 6: THE MICROPOLITICAL
In a time of fragile peace, war continues, resilient, by other means. Social breakdown has left Peljhan and many artists of his generation with a scepticism towards collectivity as a political strategy. 'If you have a cluster of micro-engagements, I think those will be ever more powerful than large demonstrations because large demonstration is theatre. It's playing roles. It's scripted space.' If the political implications of survivalist logic are unstable, ready to be rearticulated node by node, hub by hub, network by network, what is certain is that the micropolitics of shelter, defence, hibernation and protection, have, over the last decade, inspired a new functional aesthetic among artists. Artists now operate as designers, creating mobile architecture that directly intensifies social experience. Contemporary artworks such as Rotterdam based Atelier Van Lieshout's libidinal La Bais-o-Drome, Copenhagen based N55's Spaceframe & Floating Platform, New Yorker Andrea Zittel's A-Z Escape Vehicles and Paris based Studio Orta's Modular Architecture all function as living units that encourage experimentation with social security. Studio Orta in fact created modular clothing for Makrolab's 1999 Australia project. In a further step, both AVL's AVLVille and Andrea Zittel's Pocket Property have established micro-cities,

into a corner to pick the scab on my arm. Rob goes back down to the Bothy alone. Fraser heats up some pasta on a camping stove in the dysfunctional toilet area. Marko and Matevz say they don't have any time to eat, but we force them to eat some pasta; they have not eaten all day. Marko hastily rigs up an antennae.

By 11pm most things are almost working (which means they are not working), and the Slovenians leave. Marko will come back on Tuesday but Matevz has national service. We resign ourselves to shitting out in the rain.

SATURDAY 25.05.02
I wake at 10.30 feeling fatigued, and set about finding and un-velcroing windows hidden in the silver lining of the Makrolab. Matthew spends a couple of hours trying to rig up the water, with no success. As Ania and I wash up in the river she says, "The only important thing is to meet people – nice people – the rest doesn't matter", and I get this funny feeling that I get, like blushing, when someone says something which strikes me as absolutely true.
Fraser presses the wrong button on his chair and it folds up on him. The acoustics mean that if you shout from the workstations a person half way down the module won't hear you. I

12

islands for new types of artificial life. Makrolab's distinctiveness lies in it's obsessive elaboration of this aesthetic of voluntary survivalism. At its core, Makrolab can be understood as a pilot study for testing the implications of micropolitical activity. This notion is neatly defined in Peljhan's Insulation/Isolation Lecture as an ongoing, 10 year experimentation with the thesis that 'individuals in a restricted, intensive isolation can produce more evolutionary code than large social movements of great geographical and political extent.' This equation, distilled from the experience of war, simultaneously creates the terms for the stylisation and the output of life. Each Makrolab mission sets the framework for the actualisation of this hypothesis. The peculiar excitement of the Lab can be located precisely at this point. Peljhan abbreviates the core values of the project into a thesis that is dramatized through an investment in a shared experience. The participant takes on the invitation to gamble with their existence in a hypothesis about life. To become a Makronaut thus implies a propositional attitude that rolls the dice in order to act upon the prospective conditions of what an intensive life might be. In this sense, then, Makrolab is a conditional project without guarantees. It can be understood as a materialised thought experiment or 'a statement that has no power.' Peljhan explains, ' I've heard that said to me like 'Yeah it's a beautiful project and all that but actually what are you doing with it? You will not be able to do anything. Things are unchangeable unless you mobilise large masses.' Well, I don't believe in this. Actually, larger power systems have already changed. They do not operate en masse in the modern democracy. The micropolitical can never take over what we perceive as the macropolitical and its better that it doesn't. It's always good that it sort of inputs signals and solutions on a micro level. If they will be effective, they will affect maybe a community or two or three or four.'

SCALE 7: THE PROJECT
Think back to Peljhan's equation for output. 'Individuals in a restricted, intensive isolation can produce more evolutionary code than large social movements of great geographical and political extent.' What does evolutionary code mean here? Peljhan's definition seems vague. 'I just think that what I mean by code is a certain kind of output, a certain kind of result that remains there, that remains in the environment, actually in the space and exists as an idea and it's picked up later and it sort of develops. It spreads. It is the basic principle of people communicating in a very intense manner, people from different fields. For evolution you always need a synergy of forces and I use the word evolution because it's sort of the opposite of revolution. It's sort of a slower constructive change whereas revolution is probably destructive and quicker.' Why is evolutionary code such a critical yet ambiguous term? Because it is a way of articulating the production of research and of informal subjectivity as output. Evolutionary code is a term that draws together information and experience, organisation of data and development of group consciousness. It says that both are produced as relational fields to be adapted and used. Not one, or the other, but both, at once. It is the twin imperatives and their children too.

eventually manage to press the correct section of chair to unlock him. You have to be really feisty with these things says Fraser. All the chairs are left-handed except the one nearest the radio equipment. This is irritating as we are all right handed. Rob suddenly appears, bringing some camping gas and a part required to fix the gas cooker. Matthew fixes the gas cooker. Rob invites us to go with him to watch the estate army parade. The estate is allowed to keep an army; it is the only private army in Europe. We all decline the invitation to attend the parade. The radio equipment does not work; a part is missing. In the afternoon Matthew and Fraser head out to Perth to buy the part and a shameless food shop wish-list that we have drawn up. Ania tidies up. Ania says it is frightening not to be able to see your environment in London — not to have information. She says that remote areas like this have a wealth of information available — you can know EVERYTHING, but the

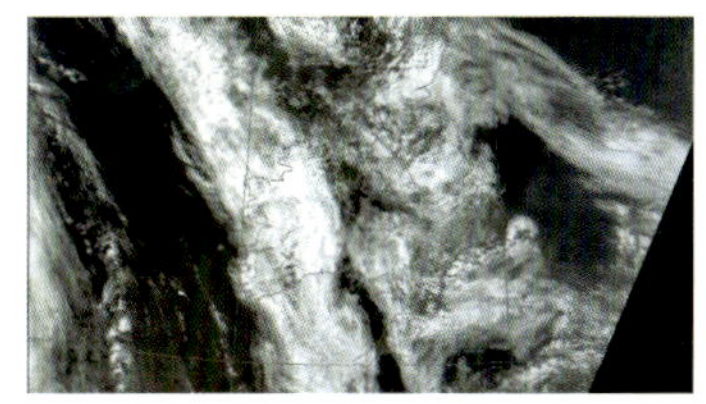

Makrolab's Twin Imperatives and Their Children Too
Kodwo Eshun

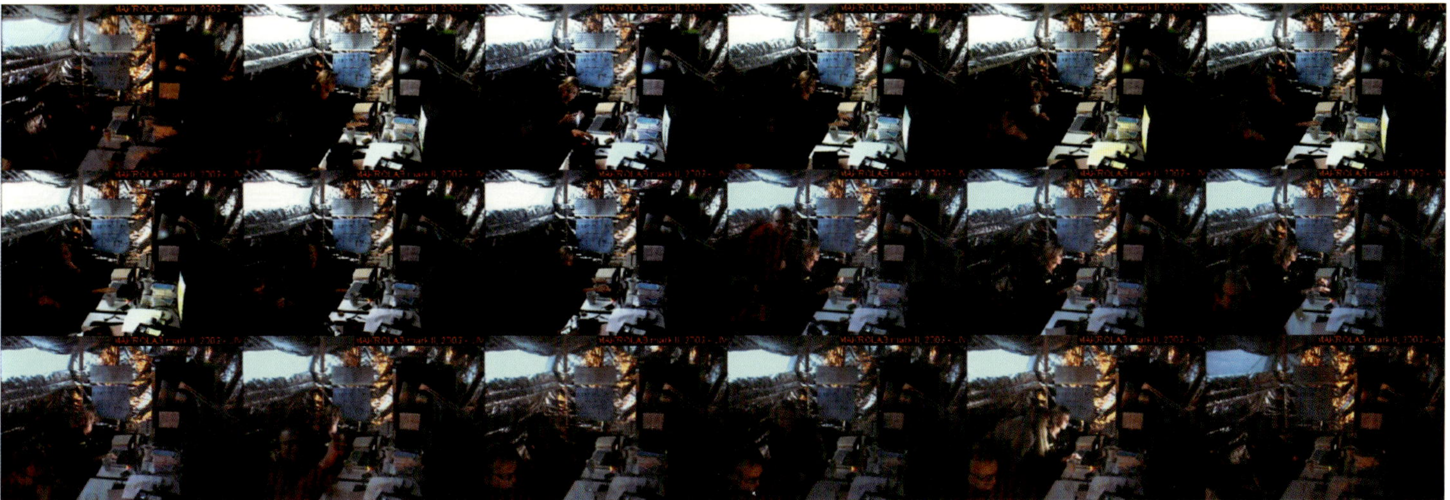

Perhaps the term 'project' acts as a shorthand for this tendency towards multiplication. Instead of producing a specific object, the artists and scientists resident at Makrolab tend to generate projects. Taking the work produced by the crew as a whole, we can say that the project agenda assumes the form of specialised data that looks, reads, displays and presents itself as documentation. Artwork becomes indistinguishable from documentation and presented from the ongoing project. Today, more and more art tends towards the condition of the project. In his essay Art In the Age of Biopolitics: From Artwork to Art Documentation, the Russian critic Boris Groys explains this turn towards 'art as documentation' as the necessary corollary of art understood as 'a form of life'. 'In the case of documentation as an artform,' he writes, 'it is not the making of any finished artwork that is documented. Rather, documentation becomes the sole result of art which is understood as a form of life, a duration, a production of history.' Such an analysis is exemplified by a work like Makrolab where the microsocial interaction that exemplifies its real originality cannot be shown but must be experienced. On clicking through the projects logged at the Arts Catalyst website during the Blair Atholl mission, it is clear that we are in the presence of 'art as documentation', in the realm of sci-art that can be identified through its emphasis on organization of data. Makrolab projects tend to take the form of fields of data. They exemplify the approach music critic Philip Sherburne calls the 'dataesthetic.' The dataesthetic can be identified in contemporary works

environments that we all inhabit; the cities, remain invisible. We don't see what is behind walls, we don't know who owns land plots. I realise I take this blindness for granted; like a good British citizen.
Ania shows me the satellite images of the Tatra mountains that she works with. They are pink and aqua, with the lakes in black; a blend of infrared imaging with the visual light range. She points out to me how vegetation comes out pink, how you can see individual trees, how detailed the information is. They are really beautiful.
Suddenly I like the Makrolab. It has a beautifully functional feel about it; which though we know is little more than a veneer, is still very comforting. We have soup for supper and stay up until 3am putting together the little plastic things you get in Kinder Surprise. Matthew got them in Perth. He tells us that some German friends once sent him a case of 144 Kinder Surprise and there were almost no duplications.

I like the lab more and more. As I write Matthew is fiddling with radio signals to my left, Fraser is to my right downloading images from the helicopter ride this afternoon and Ania is making tracings from satellite images at the kitchen table. Betalounge is loud and clear. I feel as

Makrolab's Twin Imperatives and Their Children Too
Kodwo Eshun

that seek to materialise the invisible dimensions of data—richness. In so doing, they hope to immerse the insensible and impervious viewer in the information networks that provide the operating systems of the planet. The dataesthetic has two opposing but complementary registers: firstly, the epic formal and secondly, the confessional informal. The former is visible in hyper-pedagogic projects like the World Monitoring Atlas of French artist duo Bureau d'Etude or the transnational projects of Vienna based World-information.org. As curator Ursula Biemann, herself a Makronaut, argues in her essay Geography and the Politics of Mobility, these works aspire to visualise 'the increasingly interconnected network of data-gathering systems'. The epic and the confessional are the modes of the double imperatives at work in Makrolab. The desire to map unmappable frequency spectrums, weather patterns and migration's paths overlaps with the potential for malfunction which is experienced as low level crisis. In the second register, the diary captures the flux of the self as it endures sheets of rain, power cuts, mud, waterlogged clothes, poor food, midges, perpetual uncertainty of the rural, the digital and the electrical.

To say that art becomes a life form, is to say that this moment by moment experience of Makrolab, in all its humdrum lackadaisicality, is where the art is. The unaesthetic, the miserable, the boring, the peaceful, the unmemorable: all this is where the art has fled. In Groy's words, 'Art becomes a life form, whereas the artwork becomes non-art, a mere documentation of this life form.' The diary and the atlas, the streaming link and the photo, everything that goes into the gallery -is documentation, material for the dataesthetic. This separation between art as life and non-art as document is the result of the mutation of art practice. It is the result of art's position within the regime of the biopolitical that characterises life in the early 21st Century. Groys argues that 'art becomes biopolitical because it begins to use artistic means to produce and document life as a pure activity. Indeed art documentation as an artform could only develop under the conditions of today's biopolitical age in which life itself has become the object of technical and artistic intervention.'

The atlas and the diary, the epic and the informal, the thesis and the gamble, information and experience, research and affect, data and risk, the satellite dish and the swarm of midges, the screen and the power cut: all these are consequences of the public and private logics that this essay has traced. And these logics in turn can be summed up as the dialectic of evolutionary code. Evolutionary code draws both logics together as output, but only within the Lab, and only under the conditions specified.

Within its restricted economy then, Makrolab produces an expansive subjectivity that gathers the technical, the emotional, the informational and the intuitive onto the same plane of immanence. A plane in which everything, in its intensity, matters.

■

though no 4 people could work alongside each other so nicely. We had decided to visit the highland games in the castle grounds, but we all want to wash more than we want to watch caber tossing. We visit the showers in the Blair Atholl caravan park. It takes a lot of coaxing to get my body out from under the shower, and even then I am one of the first back in the landrover. Overcome with the pleasure of cleanliness, we witness displays of masculinity and wealth; uniforms, caber tossing, bizarrely ostentatious socks and terriers. Our pleasure over-reaches itself when we splash out on venison softies. Matthew is almost beside himself with excitement; 'men in kilts! puppies! bagpipes! candy floss!' We find Rob in the bar chatting with the private army who have unbelievably frilly uniforms. Rob has spotted a stall selling 5 minute helicopter rides and volunteers to pay for us all to fly over the Makrolab to get some images. This is an unbelievably exciting prospect

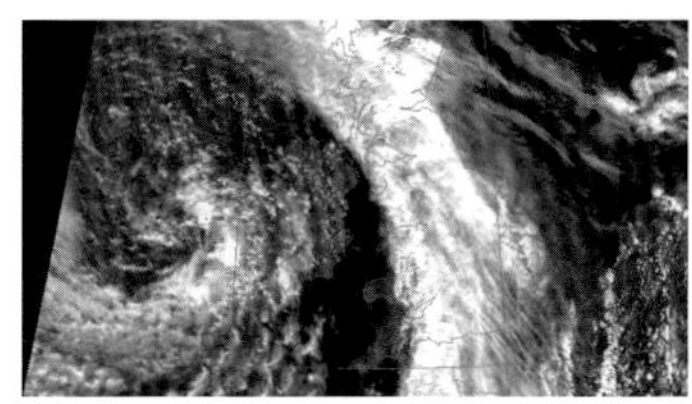

Sublime geographies, situated histories
Fraser MacDonald

The Makrolab is a *situated* project. It has its own place and its own topology. For an historical geographer, this seemingly unremarkable statement about context contains a world of meaning. There is a profound and literal sense in which Marko Peljhan's structure *takes place*; that is to say, it draws identity and purpose from operating in a particular geographical locality at a specific historical juncture. To live in the Makrolab was, for me at least, to be attuned to these geographical and historical resonances.

It is easy, of course, to define the location of the Makrolab as an abstract set of co-ordinates: NORTH 056 DEG 48' 182'', WEST 003 DEG 58' 299'', ELEVATION 1276ft. That is a position, not a place; and the place of the Makrolab is too multivariate a question to be answered by a grid reference. Let us start, then, with some toponymic referents of ascending geographical scale and allow them establish a wider context for the project: Clunes Beat; Gleann a'Chrombaidh; Atholl Estate; Highlands; Scotland.

The first of these names, Clunes Beat, reveals a geography of land use and land ownership, a 'beat' being the act of flushing game birds out of the heather and into the sportsman's line of sight. The practice of field sport in Scotland – shooting grouse and red deer – is not simply about recreation. Rather, it is part of a wider contested discourse in Scottish society regarding the ownership of (and access to) land, history and the symbols of nationhood. Shooting Scotland's charismatic macrofauna is strictly an elite affair; rightly or wrongly, it has come to epitomise the deepest class divisions in a country that might otherwise celebrate its egalitarianism. It is also a contest that cuts to the core of Scotland's self-image and international branding. These signs of national difference – tartan, heather or the red deer stag – are all disputed entities in a debate about the winners and losers of Scottish history.

One might argue that the second name, Gleann a'Chrombaidh, is a testimony to the losers. The Gaelic-speaking culture that was widespread in the eighteenth century has all but disappeared from this region. Place names on the map are its memorial. Throughout the Highlands more generally, Gaelic has been unremittingly harassed by the cultural and political dominance of the English language in the last two centuries. It is a controversial thesis, perhaps, but such attrition is by no means unrelated to the marginalisation and the ultimate clearance of the rural proletariat in the nineteenth century by the emergent capitalism of the big 'estates'. If there is a key actor here it is the clan chief turned landlord-aristocrat, a figure at the vanguard of the capitalist revolution in the Highlands at the end of the eighteenth century. And foremost amongst these families of Scottish 'nobility' were the Dukes of Atholl, whose estate remains one of the largest of its kind. Indeed, it was by kind permission of the Atholl Estate and its current proprietor that Makrolab took its place on Clunes in 2002. While this context may seem incidental to the artistic functions of the project, the Makrolab cannot be isolated from this political matrix. This, however, is a digression from my main interest.

The idea of using an innovative architectural form and the latest optical technology to dwell in, and heighten the experience of, the Atholl Estate's sublime landscape is not new. The Makrolab has an important local antecedent, built two and half centuries earlier by John Murray of Strowan (1729-1774), the 3rd Duke of Atholl. His construction, which has been variously called the Hermitage and Ossian's Hall, lies some 30 miles away on the banks of the River Braan near the village of Dunkeld. Built in 1757, the Hermitage was primarily designed as a viewing-house to

for me and absolutely removes the proceedings from English village-fete associations, triggered by of tug-of-war competitions and stalls selling sweets.
We try to explain to the stall holder where we want to be driven to. 'Sounds like Big Brother" she says, "are you going to be on TV?" I wouldn't be here if the Makrolab were TV, partly because it would appal me and partly because they wouldn't have me. I'm not very TV. Bristling with equipment we waft up the valley. The glint of the Makrolab among the dark heather makes it an easy target. The pilot banks alarmingly round the lab a few times before floating back over the hills to the castle. Helicopter flying is like dangling on a string, or being under water; you don't feel acceleration. It's much more disembodied than aeroplane travel. Reluctant to leave the beer and the softies, we are almost the last to leave the games. When we return to the landrover we find "I Love England" written in the dirt on the back fender. This disturbs Fraser ENORMOUSLY, being a Scottish socialist. He thinks we are being mistaken for shooting tenants. The rest of us don't especially care. Back in the Makrolab we work, but by 1am I am tired of the continual cold. I climb into my bunk to read "Who Owns

16

intensify the aesthetic appreciation of the Black Linn Falls which drops in spectacular cascades in front of its large bay window. Its construction was a timely engagement with eighteenth century aesthetic theory — epitomised by Edmund Burke's treatise on 'the sublime and the beautiful' published that same year — in which the bourgeois male subject ventured in search of an emotional experience of awe, exhilaration and 'a delightful horror'. Any encounter with terror, pain or danger (as long as it was not itself life-threatening) could be a source of the sublime. The wilder guises of Highland nature afforded ample opportunity and the Black Linn waterfall was quickly established as an iconic sight on the itinerary of early Scottish tourism.

The Makrolab is plainly not another Hermitage. But there are nevertheless some striking points of rapport between the two sites that bridge an historical gap of 250 years and provide the substance for my own rather phenomenological research at the Makrolab. In this sense, my residency is concerned with the performance of historiography, in which the production of historical and geographical knowledge arises out of an everyday experience of inhabiting these two sites. Writing Scottish history is conventionally a linear and empiricist enterprise, constructing narratives full of causation and order in which one monumental event neatly follows from another. Departing from this epistemology, I choose instead to adopt Walter Benjamin's injunction to 'telescope the past through the present', an idea which suggests a nesting of space and time, past and present. It is a suitably optical metaphor for the comparative study of two structures for looking.

The Hermitage represents a threshold: between Highlands and Lowlands; between the picturesque and the sublime; and between gothic gloom and enlightened modernity. Divided into two rooms, eighteenth century visitors were first ushered into a dark antechamber where they would contemplate the figure of Ossian, the great blind bard of Scottish mythology. After an appropriate interval of suspense and delay, their feelings of melancholy were turned into awe when the painted door panel vanished to reveal the overwhelming

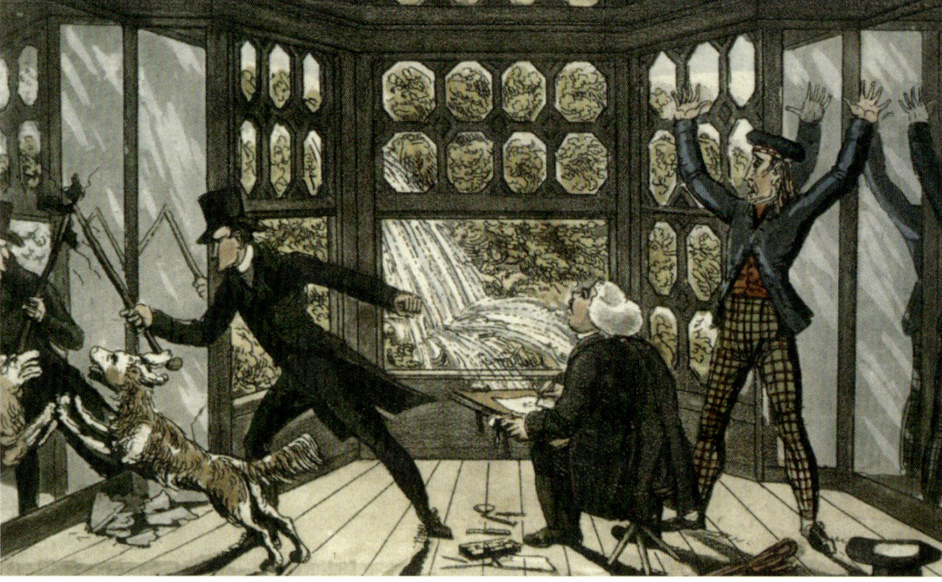

Scotland Now?" by a man called Auslan, which was published 2 years ago. On the cover is a photograph of two shooting tenants in their tweeds and deer-stalkers, with walking stick and field telescope. The top 20 landowners in Scotland are listed. The Atholl Estate comes in at no. 6 with 130,000 acres, after the Forestry Commission, the Rural Affairs Dept, the National Trust, an electricity generation plant, and Lord Dalkeith (not in that order). Auslan says "It must be wrong that so much of Scotland is run at an annual loss by rich men who can afford to subsidise country sports." He points out that the desolate landscape surrounding the Makrolab is a direct result of the estate economy which relies on income from 7 weeks deerstalking to subsidise a whole year (This is why the lab must come down at the end of July). Deer are kept in numbers far beyond the carrying capacity of the land, and devour everything; hence the boggy moonscape we live in. On

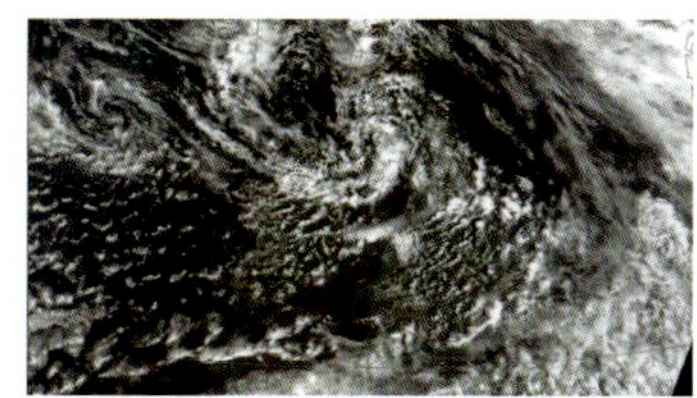

Sublime geographies, situated histories
Fraser MacDonald

brightness and tumult of the waterfall, reflected randomly in the adjacent mirror-lined hall. Here the smallness of the observant subject was radically juxtaposed with the charisma and vastness of a seemingly unknowable and untamed nature, albeit mediated by the latest optical technology. In a pre-photographic age, it heralded a new era in which lenses outside the human body would reorganise the perception of the Scottish landscape.

Although situated in the same locality, the Makrolab offers a different encounter with the sublime. Nature at the millennium is no longer the fund of awe that it once was. We now have to look elsewhere for a 'delightful horror'; it is, moreover, increasingly hard to obtain. In August 1994 on the Hebridean island of Jura – one of the canonical sites for early sublime-seekers – artist-musicians Bill Drummond and Jimmy Cauty of The KLF reputedly burnt one million pounds in fifty pound notes ("It wasn't to destroy the money" Drummond later commented, "it was to watch it burn"). Unsurprisingly, the landscape was incidental to their experience.

For the Makrolab to be sited in a remote and elemental corner of the Scottish Highlands was a formative characteristic of the project. But in a sense it was not the scenery but the structure's embeddedness in global media and communications networks that emotionally challenged the participant subject. At the interface of the workstation, the crew were pitched on the precipice of a vast information void, satellite receivers presenting a window onto a limitless torrent of moving pictures and disembodied voices.

As with the Hermitage – where the purity of the experience could be interrupted by a restive animal – life in the Makrolab was sometimes more about bathos than sublimity. At times it vacillated absurdly between the two: between the exhilaration of high-tech connectedness and the mundane discomforts of cold and damp. But such structures are important. John Murray of Strowan would have celebrated Peljhan's machine for looking and living.

■

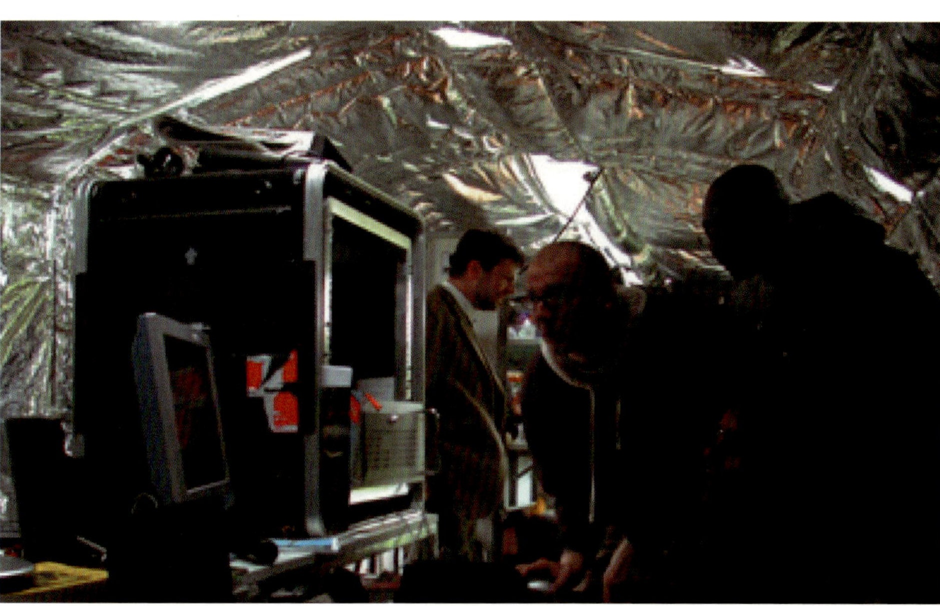

the estate there are 8,500 deer. Fraser says that across Scotland there are 300,000 deer. The carrying capacity of the land is calculated at 175,000 deer.

MONDAY 27.05.02
We have a kettle now. It leaks and lives on the floor near the front door. When it is switched on everything else loses power, so it effectively doubles up as a dimmer switch. The power drop that results from the kettle plus the compressor makes Ania's computer crash mid-long operation.
Fraser and I head over to Dunkeld to document the Hermitage, dropping Ania off to copy maps at the Estate office. Matthew stays at the lab. Fraser takes shots of the waterfall while I amuse myself by filming couples who have come to pet each other. I am amazed that this canonically Romantic spot is still associated with romance in the most basic way.
We return at 5ish to find Matthew without internet. A storm at noon caused static to build up in the lab, which is built as a Faraday cage. The only objects not earthed are the radio and external frame of one of the PC's. Because Matthew was online his Mac was directly connected to the kit. He got a few shocks through his metal keyboard and looked up to see

Nature Pollutes Culture Pollutes Nature
Helen Evans

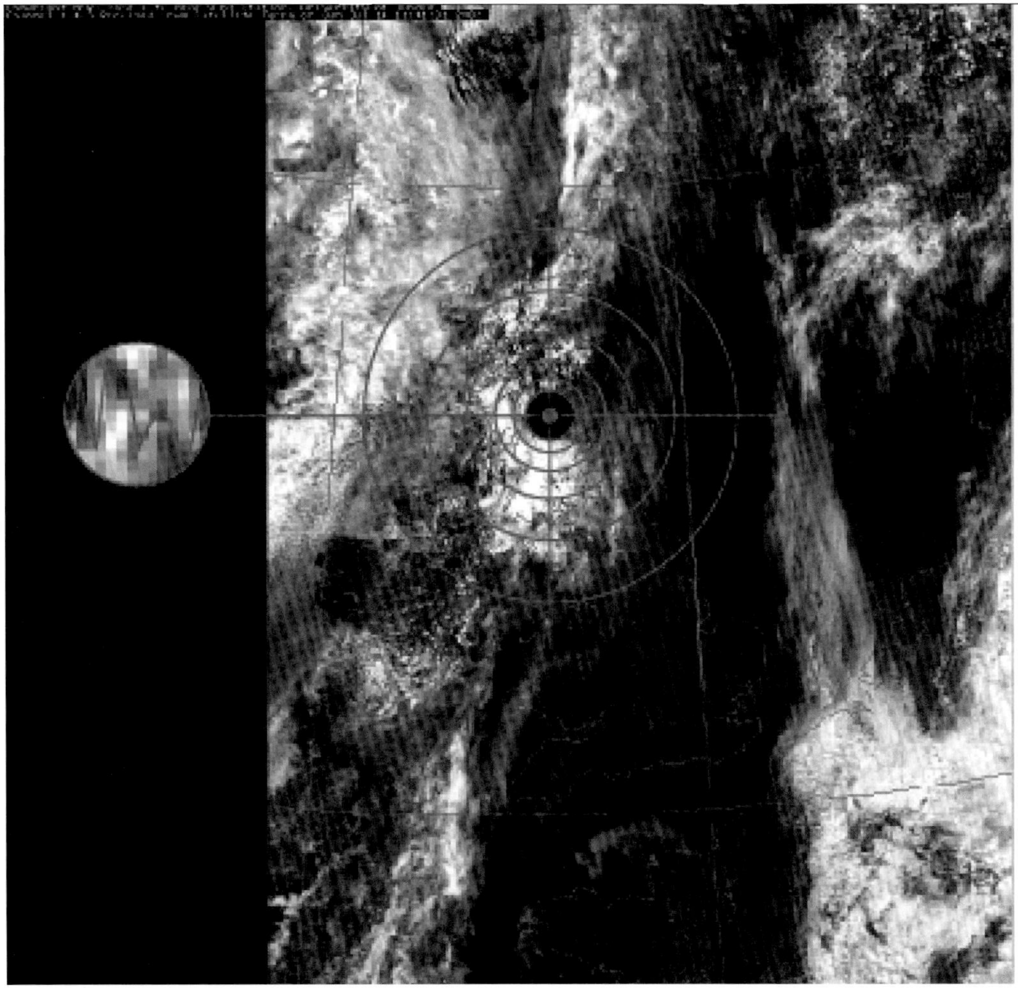

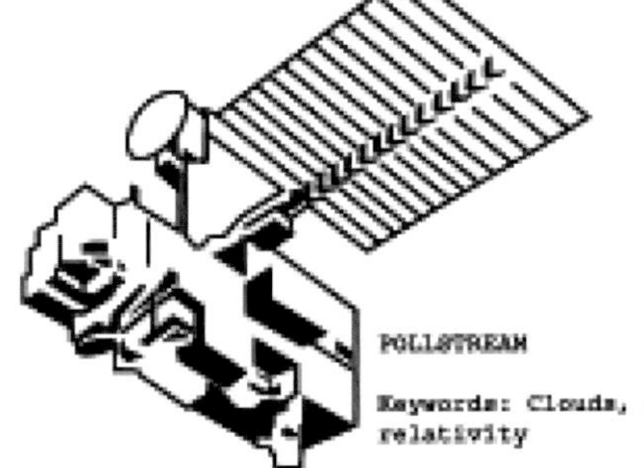

electricity arcing across from the radio in front of him. The arcing didn't stop until he pulled out the antennae with a pair of rubber-handled pliers. The lightning seems to have blown the router; so we are without ethernet, and Matthew can't work. This is particularly cruel because all Matthew seems to do is try to fix stuff. He's far less incompetent that the rest of us. Now he's spent an afternoon trying to fix the ethernet. I think of Matthew as a good-tempered and patient man, but he's struggling to hang onto this version of himself. I wonder what he will do if he can't hold onto his nice self in adversity. I have had an idea for a video, which will require a few props and the assistance of Matthew and Rob. I mainly need to locate some golf clubs so in the evening I make the long drive down in the landrover to ask Ronnie the gamekeeper, if I can borrow his golf clubs. Ronnie comes to the door in the most outrageous pair of sage herringbone plus-fours.

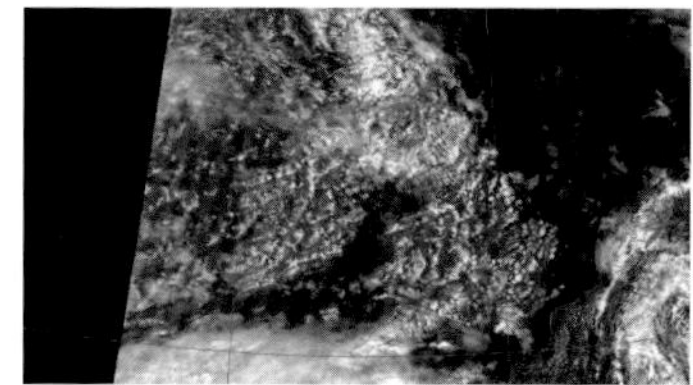

Nature Pollutes Culture Pollutes Nature
Helen Evans

Above us, rotating around the globe, thousands of data packages are beaming back and forth, are counted, calculated, manipulated and thrown into the ever filling data banks of global atmospheric modelling systems. Manmade materials, signals and codes permeate space, both near and far. Yet seldom do we think of this rich mix spinning around above us — since we have few means to access it.

The current software prototype: Pollstreamv.01 (built in Makrolab), displays, analyses and recodes images of cloud cover over Blair Atholl, taken during the residency by the NASA satellite TERRA (EOS AM-1) with MODIS (Moderate Resolution Imaging Spectroradiometer). The software pinpoints the position of Makrolab, enlarges the image to maximum resolution and scans each pixel's brightness. The software is able to generate and distort an audio collage according to the daily cloud patterns over Scotland using Makrolab's AR5000 wideband radio receiver mixing natural or unknown radio frequencies, air traffic control, aeronautical and meteorological codes, mobile telephone calls and utility radio transmissions.

Depending upon the pattern generated by the cloud cover on a particular day, the radio samples will vary in pitch, speed, phase shift, modulation and duration. Other audio signals use an algorithm to generate sound waves according to the cloud pattern.

In Pollstream v.01, as in the geophysical world, the clouds interact, pollute, alter and distort audio channels as well as generate their own noises: The higher the density of the cloud, the higher the pitch and speed of the audio signal that is reflected. Heavy precipitation may cause a strong signal to reduce for a relatively short time and phase shifting. A cloud suspected of carrying an electrical charge will generate a high level of frequency interference and audio scattering.

The question is not simply, what might pollution sound like but also, how can one define pollution within the electromagnetic spectrum? Is it nature that is polluting culture or the other way around?

The target is to develop free open source software that can decode atmospheric satellite data measuring Co2, aerosol and radiation from a specific location and make this data accessible to non experts, across all platforms. This tool means that the invisible space of data flows can be materialised, given a structure, poetics, and a politics.

www.hehe.org/pollstream

■

Fantastic. He says he'll lend me a few clubs and asks how we are up at the Makrolab. When I say wet he laughs uproariously. On the way back up to the lab I pick up a new inhabitant called Ewan from Paris. He says he is a meterologist, but he has come with a French beginner's guide to weather, and a 19th century lens contraption to measure the intervals of sunshine by burning lines in bits of paper — which is incredibly un-Makrolab, so we doubt him a bit.

The four of us work concertedly until 1am. Ewan is clearly puzzled by our determination. He goes for a quick walk in the twilight, and returns to say that when he got to the track a huge herd of 'creatures' were there staring at him. That'll be the red deer I say. I wonder how much excitement there can be in shooting something so easy to hit.

TUESDAY 28.05.02
There seems to be no hope of fixing the ethernet, so we all (save Ewan) accompany Ania on a field trip. We drive the landrover to Loch Moraig and set off toward Carn Liath on Beinn a Ghlo.

I remember, while writing this that I have not seen Beinn a Ghlo clear of cloud once during my time here, yet as we walked briskly toward the massif I firmly believed that the cloud cap

Landing Strip for Insects
Tim Knowles

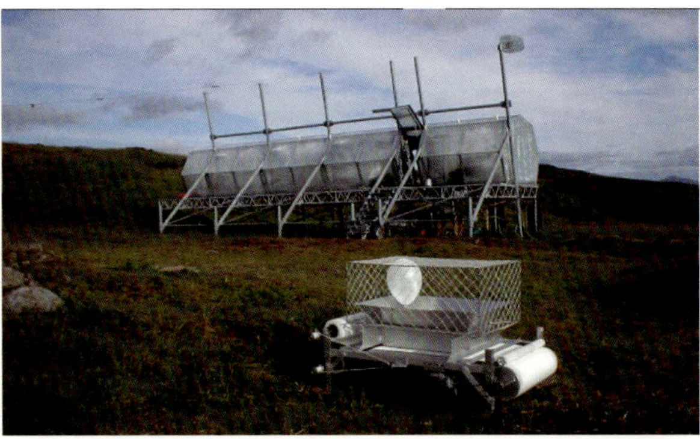

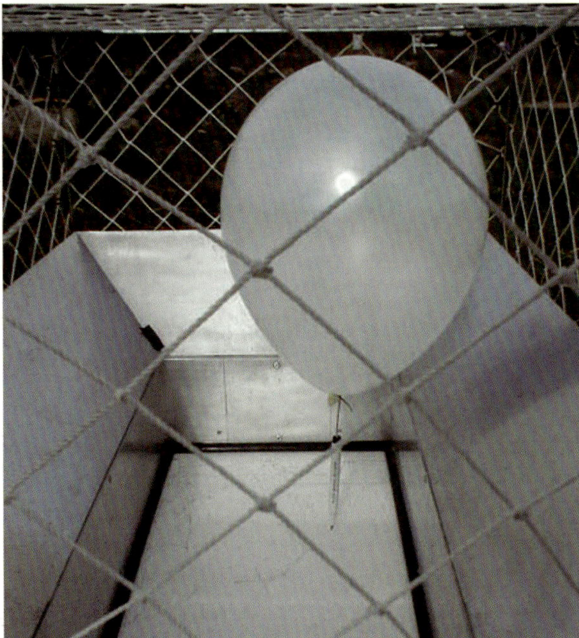

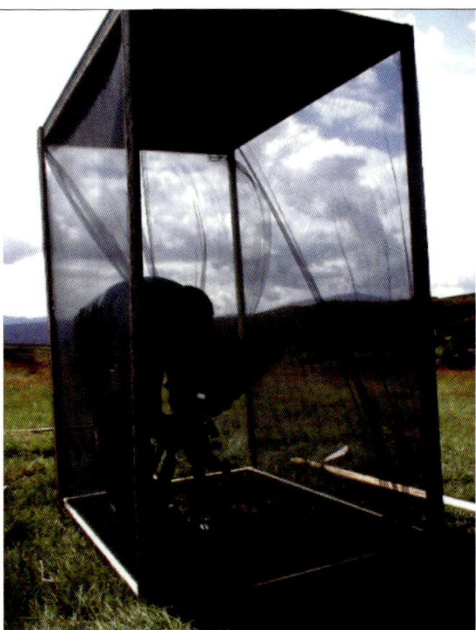

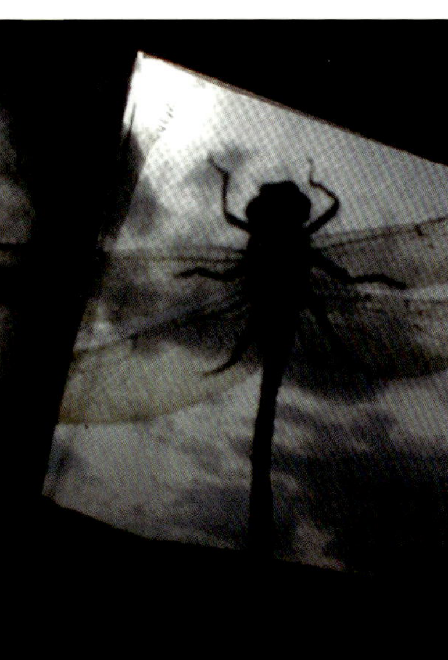

Balloon drawings are produced as a result of the wind's effects on a buoyant helium balloon, from which a pen is suspended [nib on paper]. As the balloon is blown around by the wind within the confines of a cage, the pen traces its path across a sheet of paper, its movement limited to an area of the paper by a vertical frame. The result is a mixture of scratchy lines, elegant curves, spreading blots and dense scribbles which record the winds effects on the balloon at a specific time and space.

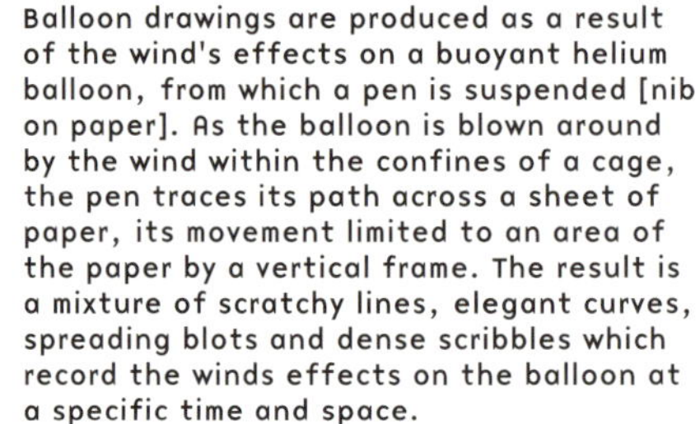

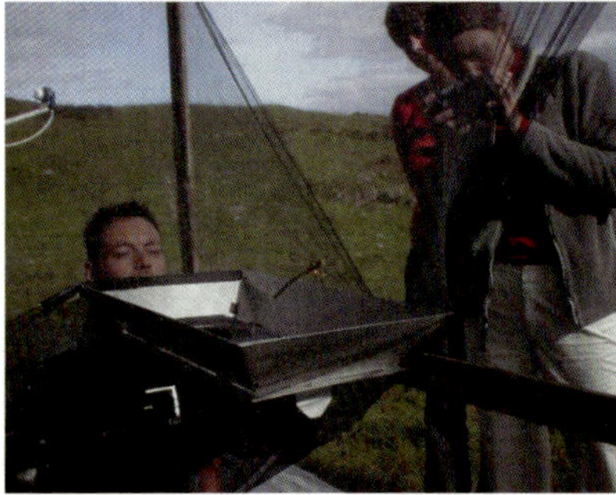

would lift. We are about a third of the way up when a storm springs up – a really nasty one. The rain drives horizontally from our right. It's intensely cold. We are all soaked immediately and make feeble jokes about the 'sunny intervals' flirtatiously hinted at by weather reports. We keep climbing into the cloud. It goes dark. We keep climbing. On a cairn at about 960m the others balance against the wind, arms outstretched. I watch them in the milky darkness and sulkily refuse to join in, complaining that I can't sympathise with an urge to get to the TOP of anything. I cheer up on the way down, but I am sick with cold by the time we arrive back at the lab to pick up dry clothes before heading back to the caravan site for a shower. At the caravan site I put all my clothes in the dryer, as I have no dry clothes left whatsoever, and walk to the shower block in a vest and a skirt that I packed in the anticipation of summer. We all shower and then in a

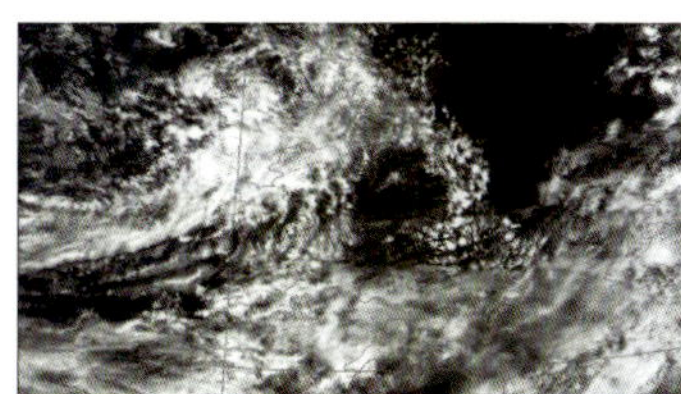

Landing Strip for Insects
Tim Knowles

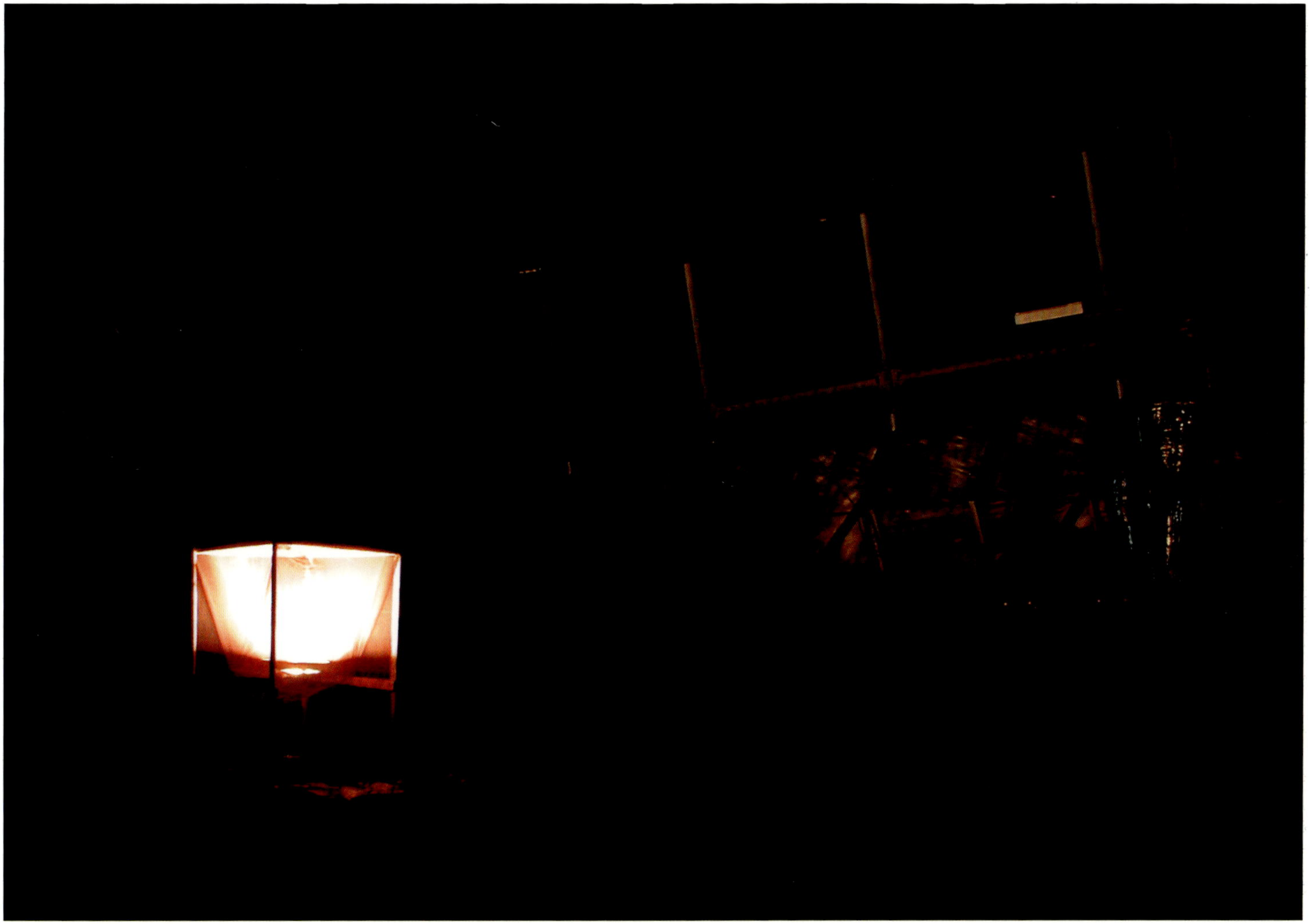

reckless ecstasy of physical pleasure we drive to a cafe and order pasta and icecream. Walking back down the boggy slope to the Makrolab in the evening, clean, dry, and NOT HUNGRY, I slip and drop my bundle of dry clothes, once again soaking the set of clothes that I am wearing. Ewan tries to show me the results of his sun-measuring device but the paper is so wet that it has turned to pulp and can't even be prised out of it's holder. It looks unsinged to me. At 9ish I am trying to call Rob about tomorrow's shoot when Rob and Zoe arrive with a bottle of wine to tell us that the nearest mobile phone mast was struck by lightning at 2pm; so we are ENTIRELY cut off now. They also tell us that Marko has missed his plane due to a bad connection in Italy. We are not surprised. You must by now think that I am making this up. It's wildly improbable that so much can go wrong; but it has. However, the golf clubs that I requested from Ronnie the game keeper, have arrived. There is a lovely yellow 'Blair Atholl 1976' sticker on the side of the canvas bag. I fall asleep to the sound of an almighty storm.

WEDNESDAY 29.05.02
Today is a day for filming; this is to make a video for an exhibition called GOLF at the Standpoint Gallery, which

Landing Strip for Insects
Tim Knowles

ZZ

Insect Flight Path studies examine in great detail the varying characteristics of different species of insect, aiming to produce a range of unique, varied images.

These long exposure photographs capture the elegant and erratic patterns of insects in flight, and follows on from previous works which explored movement and the use of chance or processes beyond the artists control.

To do this a net sided frame in which insects could be photographed was constructed with a black velvet panel at the top [to create a matt black background]. The camera and halogen lamp are mounted in a unit on a tripod within the net frame. Different captured insects could then be placed in the frame to be photographed. The netted frame ensured the insects could not escape and served to restrict their area of flight.

A light situated beside the camera [shutter open], aims up into the night sky[or a black velvet cloth], insects attracted by the light, fly chaotically across and around the cameras field of view, their erratic paths and wing movements are left as a ghostly flame or fern like trail of orange light recorded onto the negative.

The different insects, with their various forms and types of flight leave their individual trails – a Daddy Long legs leaving a spindly or hairy trail, a small moth – a smoke like wisp and a larger moth or butterfly – a fern like pattern.

Insects caught were:
Golden-ringed Dragonfly
[cordulegaster boltonii]
Small Heath Butterflies
[coenonympha pamphilus]
Muslin Moths
[diaphora mendicca]

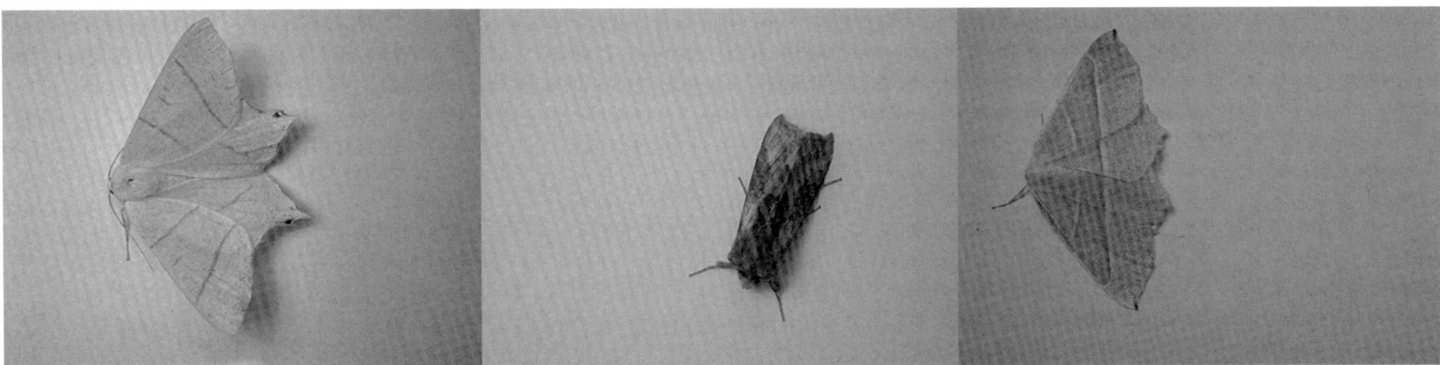

I should not be working on really as I'm meant to be working for Contemplation Room, but I can't resist the opportunity. During an enormous downpour in Pitlochry I buy a deerstalker and a tweed jacket. We film easily — Matthew and Rob are naturally perfect in their roles, and extremely good natured about being asked to scramble up and down banks. I feel grateful and happy, despite Matthew having lost all Ronnie's golf balls. Something feels as if it's gone well.

In the afternoon I return to the Makrolab to watch the footage and find Ewan still trying to record sunny intervals in the rain. The golf footage is great — better than I thought. Matthew becomes fond of the deerstalker prop and buys it from me. He claims no one will know what it is for back in San Francisco.

Rob turns up at 6 in a furious temper, having waited for 30 minutes for Ania at the castle, so Fraser and I head back down the long estate track in

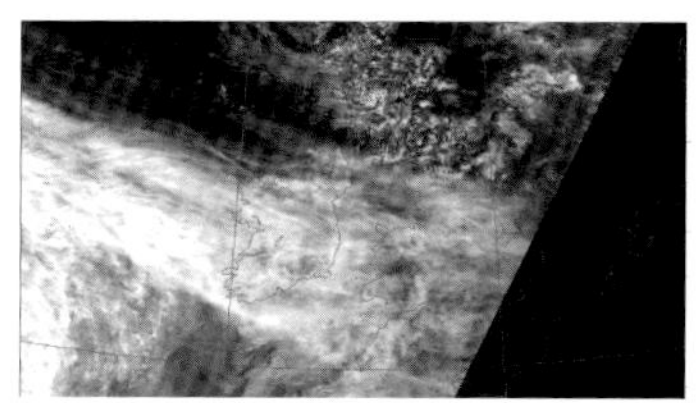

Experiments in acoustic cartography
Calum Stirling

Landstylus is a project initiated at Makrolab in 2002, which created audio journeys around the hills and glens surrounding Makrolab. The project explored the acoustic potential of the natural landscape by transforming contour data into elements of geoacoustic notation.

A process was devised to examine contour and topographical information about a specific area using digital terrain models. Using software calculations, the heightfield, land texture and slope angles were extrapolated to create midi sound maps. The 3D flythrough and sounds generated in the screenwork Landstylus Survey#2 were created from a 20km computer generated model of the hills and glens surrounding Blair Atholl and the Atholl Estate.

The project was conceived as a poetic vehicle in which to explore the mental and physical space that separates us from the natural landscape and is inspired in part by the aptly named 'Hill and Dale' audio recording process pioneered by Edison in 1910.

www.modelcitizen.org.uk

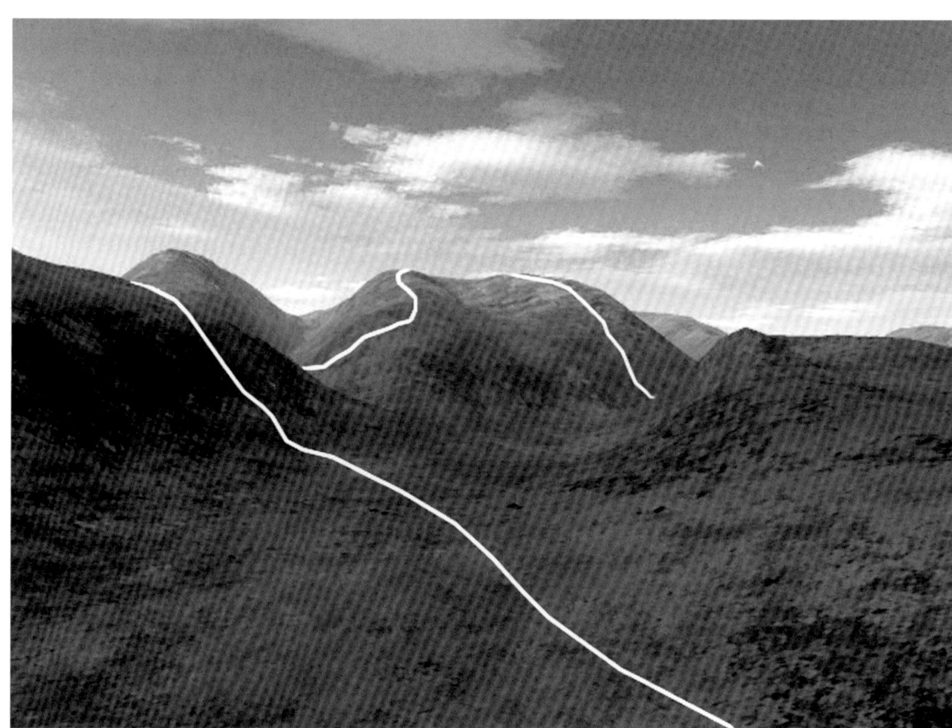

Video Still from Landstylus Survey#2

the landrover with him to fetch her. We happen across two strangers heading up our track in a 4x4. They turn out to be on their track, in fact; Sarah Troughton and her husband are on their way to pay us a visit. Fraser almost hyperventilates with horror at having to deal with aristos.

I call Ania, who says she's managed to walk as far as the car park at the House of Bruar – which is an outlet off the A9 for what Fraser calls Highland Flingery, and from which Rob averts his eyes on passing. Having located Ania in a different car park we drive back to the lab and meet the Troughtons; who are very pleasant and interested but inadvertently provoke a crisis in Fraser, who is a Marxist and feels bewildered to find himself in a situation where he is clearly required to be deferential to feudal superiors. It is a bit like a state visit, though Matthew remains buried in his keyboard and roundly ignores them.

Marko returns at 10pm. We are relieved. He says he had the first nervous breakdown of his life in an airport at noon trying to get onto a 'GO' flight. 'GO' were outstandingly rude to him and then lost all his bags.

THURSDAY 30.05.02
It was a very cold night. I wake up feeling shitty and decide I've had

Waveforms and Transmission (Making Radio)
Radioqualia

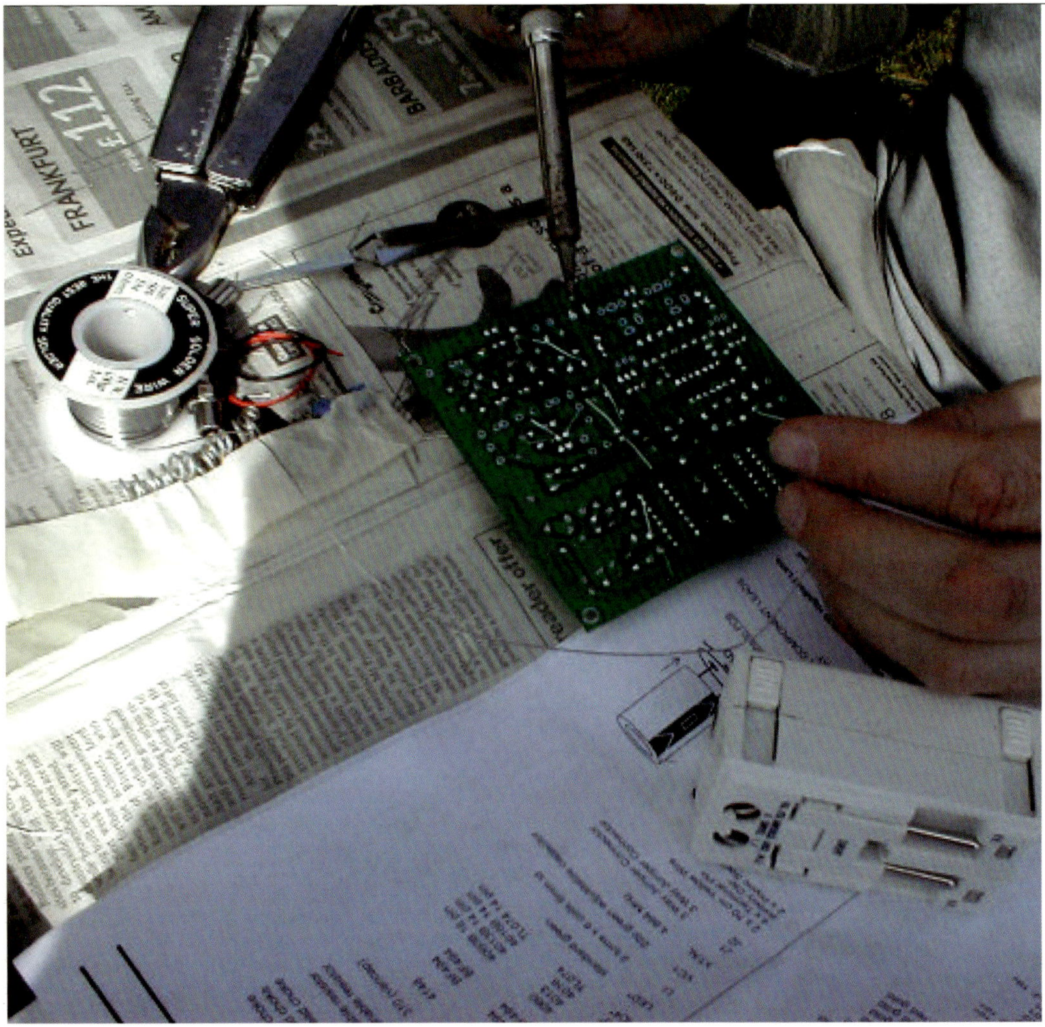

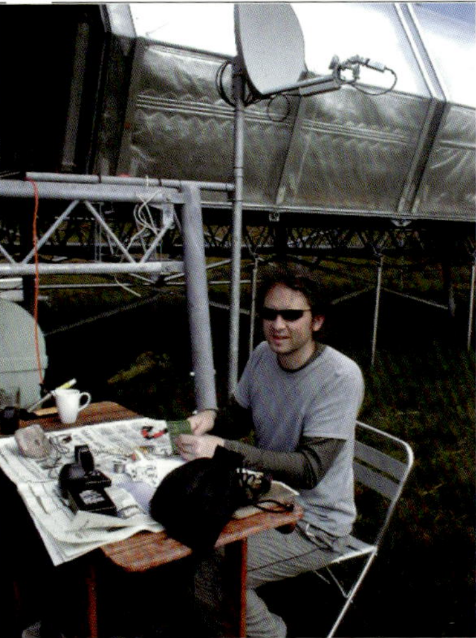

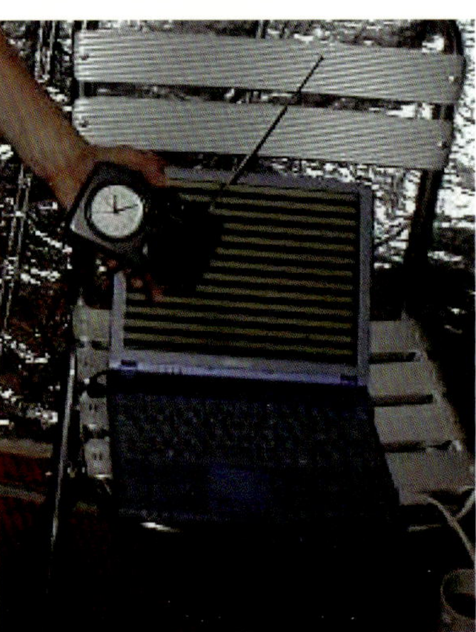

enough of feeling shitty. Well, my body decides that. The incessant rain coupled with the fact that we can't dry anything, not even ourselves once we are wet means we don't go out on the hills. This means we stay in and work at our immobilising workstations - but there are only 3 of them and 6 of us in a very small space. It's cold and claustrophobic. There is no heating and no windows. It's a really bad combination. Last night Marko fixed the ethernet so there was an email rush, which I avoided by falling asleep. Now in the morning finally accessing my emails doesn't improve my mood. In fact, it makes me remember all the other comfortable places I could be; which depresses me. In an attempt to feel normal I head down the long and appallingly bumpy track for a shower feeling utterly miserable. The shower helps but I get back to the lab to find that Matthew's mac has not recovered from the lightning strike and refuses to connect to the ethernet.

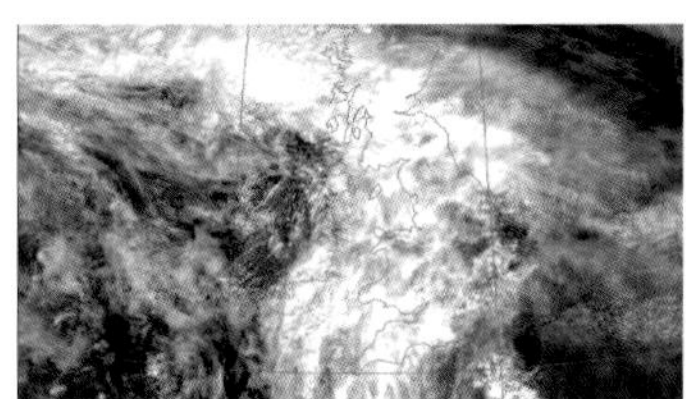

Waveforms and Transmission (Making Radio)
Radioqualia

On Thursday 18 July, r a d i o q u a l i a built a 50 milliwatt transmitter, and launched Makrolab's first FM radio station transmitting from Blair Atholl Estate in Scotland. The radio station had a broadcast range of around half a kilometre, meaning that vehicles in the area equipped with car radio would have been able to receive the signal. Makrolab106FM broadcasted regularly from 18 July to the end of makrolab operations on 28 July.

Makrolab106FM's first transmission was an audio work created by r a d i o q u a l i a. Subsequent transmissions featured sound materials captured from the internet, including lectures on cosmology by Stephen Hawking and string theorist, Tom Banks, music by net.radio stations associated with the Xchange network, and music from the personal CD collections of makrolab crew members. Makrolab106FM also received a signal from London based station, Resonance104.4FM via their internet stream. One memorable Makrolab106FM broadcast was a Resonance programme on the Autonomous Astronauts Association featuring an interview with Makrolab crew member, Ewen Chardronnet.

LISTENING TO SPACE
The weight of imagery associated with space is overwhelming. We can all look at space, in pictures on television, in books, and on the internet, but in popular culture, we have no sense of what sounds are evident in space. In film, on television, and indeed in documentary, space is usually depicted as an aural void. And indeed, most people associate space with silence.

This is in fact a misnomer. A great percentage of our scientific understanding of space has been derived by listening to space through radio telescopes. The data we glean from listening to space is every bit as significant and important to our comprehension of the Universe as more traditionally understood optical observation.

Even the scientific perception of radio astronomy is largely visual. Despite the fact that objects are observed and recorded using radio, their emissions are represented using graphs, diagrams, graphic visualisations and other visual media. Many objects, do however, emit radiation in the audible band, making it

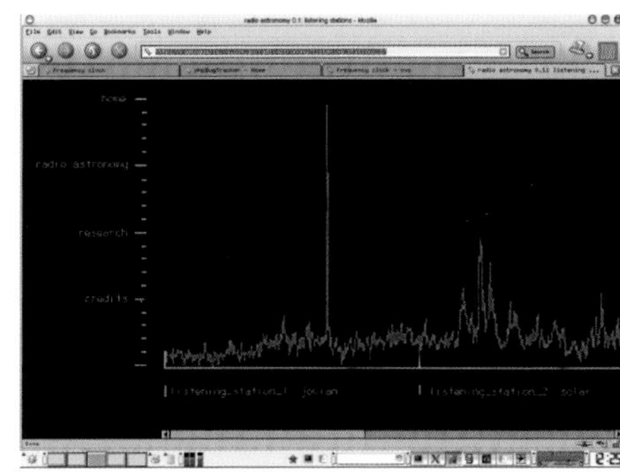
Listening Station front page

When I'm in an unusual situation like this – one that dictates your feelings in an undesirable way, I usually manage to find it interesting, but today I can't. I resort to loud betalounge through my headphones and building 3D computer models of data mountains, rendering them as icebergs. When I can't bear to build any more icebergs I look them up at weather station internet sites. When even this palls I tune into the short wave radio and listen to Manchester metroport's weather reports, and sundry other radio waves. All these things would all be fun were it a reasonable temperature in here. Eventually I retreat to my bunk, but it feels dysfunctional to go to bed in daylight, so I get up again.

At about 9pm Fraser and Ania return from their field trips and I start on the hour long walk up the estate track towards a bothy in the hills above us, where we have planned to have a fire-party. It's not raining. I lie in the heather wearing the tweed jacket that I bought from the charity shop for the filming and feel happy. There's so much space; it's absolutely quiet save for bird song and the river in the distance; the sky is ravishingly beautiful.

When I reach the bothy Fraser already has the fire going and smoke is spilling out through the chinks in the

26

possible to hear the Universe. Space, as it turns out, is a very noisy place, with each planet, star, nebula and cluster, containing its own sonic signature. And yet, very few people have ever heard space. Hardly any of us could describe the sound of a single planet or star.

Radio Astronomy is an attempt to address this. At makrolab, r a d i o q u a l i a began to create the first steps toward the creation of Radio Astronomy. At the lab, r a d i o q u a l i a made contact with a number of radio astronomers and research institutions, including the University of Hawaii Windward Community College Radio Observatory (WCCRO), Radio Jove and ex-Jodrell Bank astronomer, Gavin Starks, and began to make observations of objects in the galaxy.

At makrolab, r a d i o q u a l i a listened to, and recorded, radio storms from the planet Jupiter, as well as the output of the Sun and other highly audible and distinctive astronomical objects.

The complex interplay between the planet Jupiter and its volcanic moon, Io, produces "radio noise storms", which can be heard on the radio band from about 15 MHz up to 38 MHz. A storm can last from a few minutes to several hours. Two distinctive types of bursts can be received by radio astronomers during a storm. L-Bursts (long bursts of radiation) which sound like ocean waves breaking up on a beach. S-Bursts (short bursts of radiation) which sound like popcorn popping, or like a handful of pebbles thrown onto a tin roof.

The Sun is also a very commonly heard object via radio astronomy. When there is a solar flare on the Sun's surface, it is often accompanied by a burst of radio energy projected into space. This energy can be monitored with standard ShortWave and VHF radio receivers. Solar bursts typically last from half a minute to a couple of minutes and often sound like a rapid hissing noise followed by a gradual decrease back to the original audio level.

ELECTROMAGNETIC SURVEILLANCE
Van Eck Eavesdropping, outlined by Dutch scientist Wim van Eck described how data can be collected from computer monitors, using the monitor's electromagnetic emissions. Van Eck pointed out that computer data was more vulnerable than people expected, making the observation that surveillers did not need access to a computer's hard drive in order to observe the data and activity of a computer. Surveillers could deduce the data on a particular computer by remotely monitoring the electromagnetic output of the display screen itself. This surprising research unveiled and entirely new and covert method of electronic observation.

Van Eck Eavesdropping has been the subject of a great deal of interest in recent years, as the use of personal computers becomes ubiquitous. The US Government has identified the practice as part on a project group entitled, TEMPEST. During the 1950's, the US government has become increasingly concerned that emanations from encryption devices could be captured and then reconstructed using EM field monitoring devices. If emanations were recorded, interpreted, and then played back on a similar device, it would be extremely easy to reveal the content of an encrypted message.

Research showed it was possible to capture emanations from a distance, and as a response the TEMPEST programme was stones that make up the back wall. We chat in the little smoke-filled room while waiting for the others who are following in the landrover. With no technology in sight we cook sausages on skewers. Marko falls asleep in his chair. It feels normal. At 2am the landrover heads back full of sleepy people and empty bottles. Fraser and

I walk back over the silent moor - it's not dark; dusk still lingers in the sky. It is not raining. As we near the Makrolab French techno can be heard clearly. Inside, we find Ania asleep and all the men playing on their computers. I crawl into my sleeping bag on the top bunk and set my alarm to wake me at 6am so I have time for

a final solitary walk back to the bothy before my train leaves at 9am. When I wake it's not raining.
Abigail Reynolds
Postscript.
Immediately after leaving the lab, Ania and I made arrangements to collaborate on a video piece using her remote sensing images. Matthew

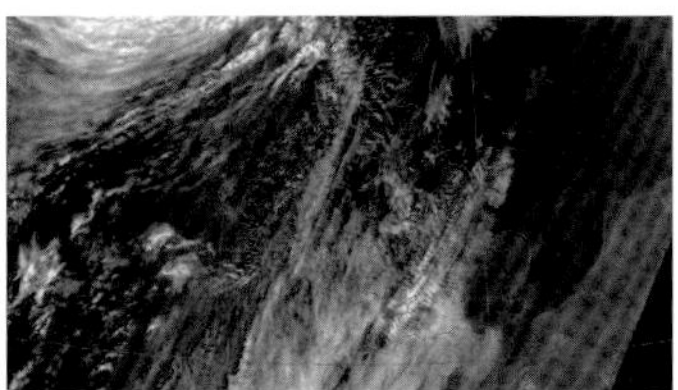

Waveforms and Transmission (Making Radio)
Radioqualia

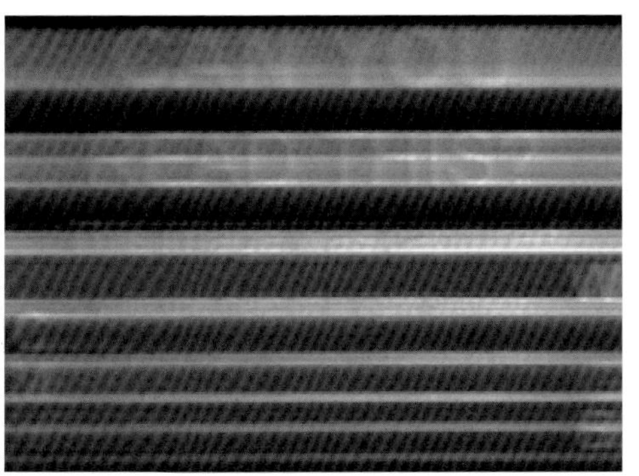

Van Eck Experiment

established. TEMPEST has developed a set of classified standards for limiting electric or electromagnetic radiation emanations from electronic equipment, and has provided advice on how to shield devices so that eavesdropping is not possible.

At the Makrolab, r a d i o q u a l i a began some practical research into the techniques and technology associated with Van Eck eavesdropping, and the ways EM-fields can be represented.

The first part of this process involved learning about the basic physics of monitor emissions. During this phase our research experimented with Tempest for Eliza, a software written by Erik Thiele that allows the control of the high frequencies emitted from a standard monitor so that the monitor can transmit intelligible data in the AM band.

Interestingly our research revealed that it has also been suggested that 'broadcasting' in the AM spectrum in this way could be used to transmit software licence keys. This would mean that code could be embedded in an application to allow the transmission of certain data through the monitor.

Microsoft has been implicated in the article, 'British Technology Might Flush out Software Pirates by John Burgess', as a leading developer using emissions in this way to combat software piracy. Although this research has apparently been halted, the idea was that Microsoft could simply drive a vehicle through any street and using emission-monitoring equipment detect which homes and businesses contained pirated software.

www.radioqualia.net
www.erikyyy.de/tempest/
http://lists.essential.org/1998/
info-policy-notes/msg00005.html

reported that his deerstalker went down a storm on the West Coast. The Makrolab project rumbled on without us, I traveled to Copenhagen and showed my videos of the Makrolab. Six months after this, I came home to find a message from Fraser on my ansaphone. His voice sounded odd. When we spoke, he asked me if I'd

checked my email, and then told me that he had received a group Makrolab email list message to the effect that Ania had been killed in a car accident in Budapest about a month after leaving the lab. This explained why she hadn't responded to my emails for the last few months.
The news that Ania was dead affected

me very strongly. I felt, and still do feel that the stupendousness of the Makrolab experience fostered in Ania, Fraser, Matthew and I an extraordinarily immediate and intimate closeness. Besides which, I really liked her. Ania had sent Fraser a series of images from the lab, and he forwarded them to me. One shows the four of us

with our arms around each others shoulders, having just emerged from our helicopter ride.
We are all grinning enormously.

MAKRODIARY 2
It had been over 2 weeks into the residency and my time was almost up. No rockets had been flown on any

Rocket Launching
Miles Chalcraft

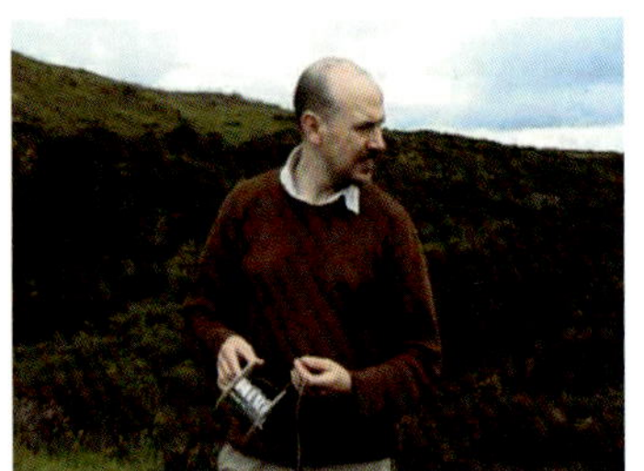

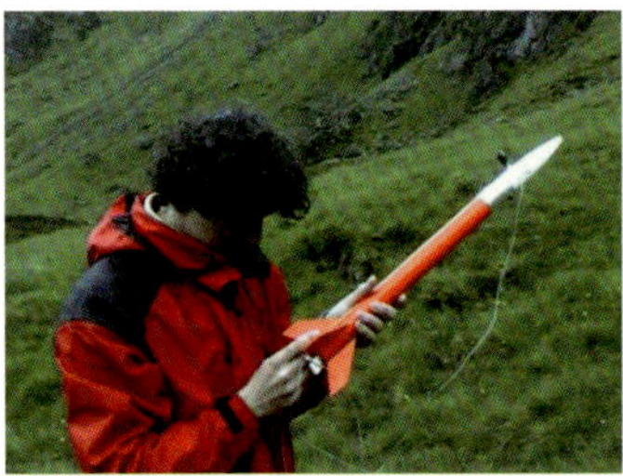

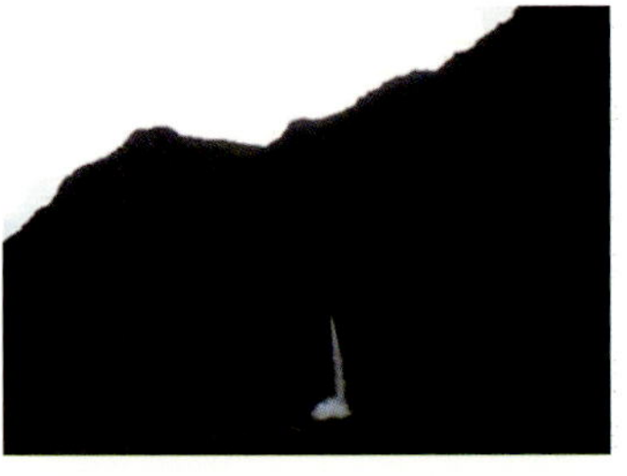

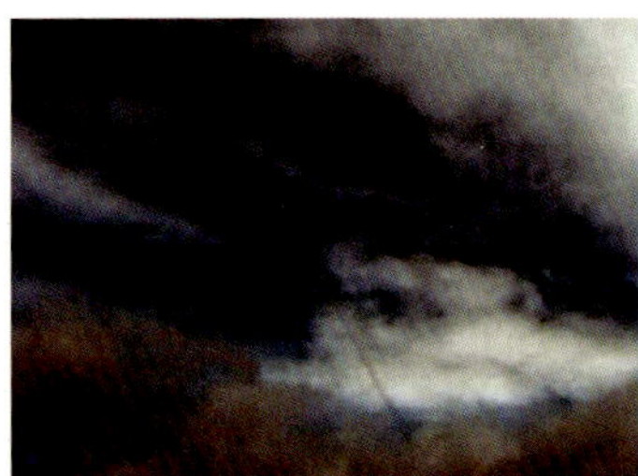

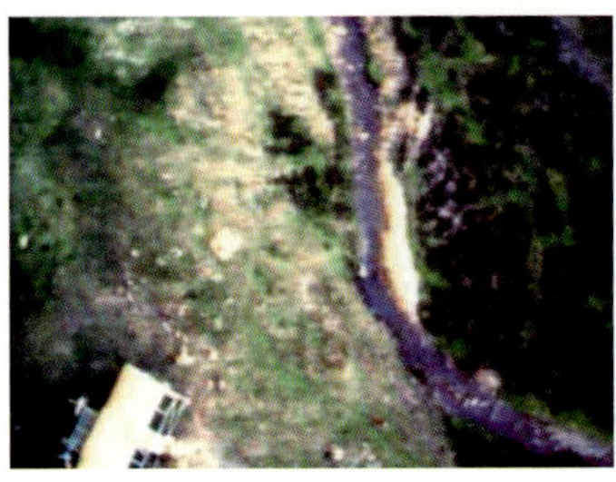

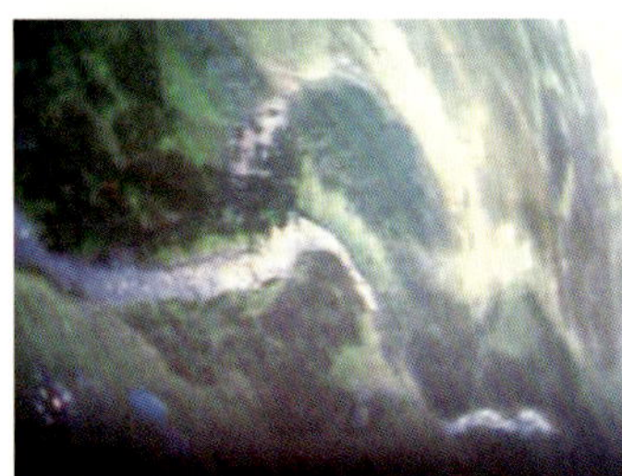

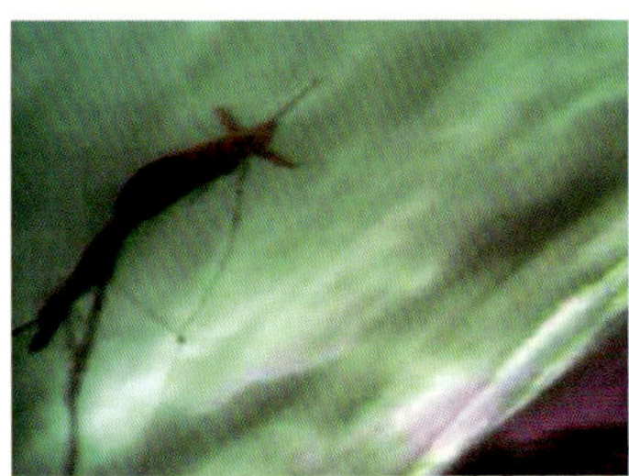

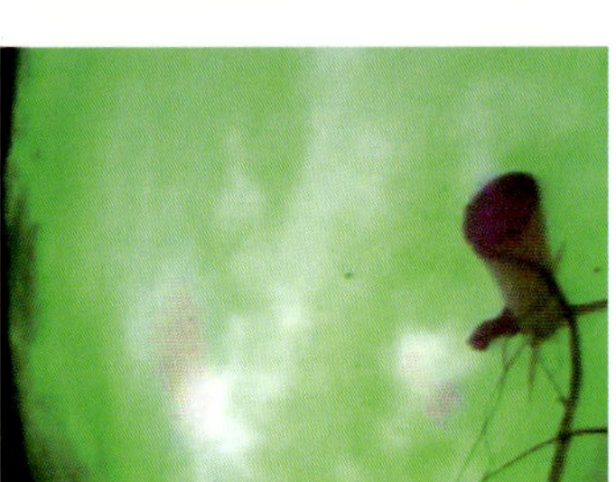

Thoughts before leaving

It won't be easy — to launch a fragile rocket from a windy mountain. It will be damned hard. Someone once said 'it's not because it is easy that we choose to go to the moon but because it is hard'. And then they were killed. Those two events weren't linked but sometimes intentions and results are combined by circumstances outside of one's interests and then you end up in trouble. Or worse... It's about when you went for a walk and luck ran out.

When luck went home without saying goodbye, tired of the mountain's relentless bad temper and went and found someone sitting comfortably infront of the TV with a small pice of paper in their hand and a trouble-free future. So it goes
Temper Temper.

And then you fell. Or drifted into blue-lipped sleep. Or panicked and ran into a nightmare of zero vision and life leaking cold. Eventually you were found and now your story is told. And that's where these rockets come in. Feeble eyewitnesses they are to where

you lay. But there you were and were you cold or were you nothing fast. I won't know for sure but I do know that a cold bed was waiting for you that night and if you could have left the ground at a speed so great as to snatch you from the jaws that lead to weeping widows would you not have done so? And warmed that bed.

mountains yet, the time having vanished in workshops, designing, building and planning. It was now or never.

We struggled up to our goal through a boulder field of rough and sandy rocks, occasionally seeing glimpses of a path to our right. I didn't want to follow it as it may have circumvented the Col that we needed to reach. The cloud was low and visibility about 50 yards when we reached the rocky plateau that was to be the first launch pad of the project. Still a little uncertain whether we had reached our intended spot we followed a thin trickle of a stream east for 10 minutes before backtracking to our original spot.

It was a bleak spot to die, but then isn't any? This was the middle of summer yet our waterproofs were wringing with the moisture from the driving mist and a wind flapped in gusts threatening worse to come. It had been still on the valley floor. By our estimations, though I admit that the evidence was sketchy, this was as

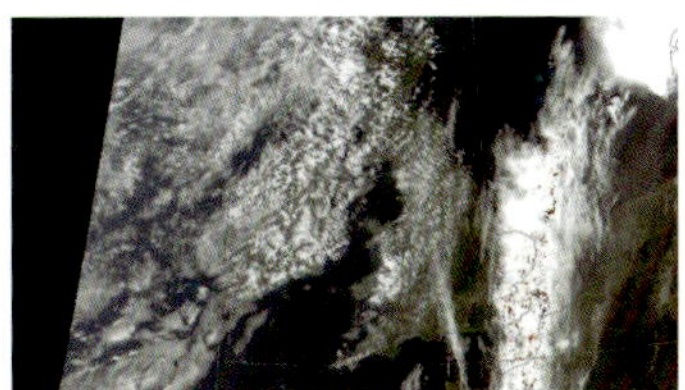

Helena Johard

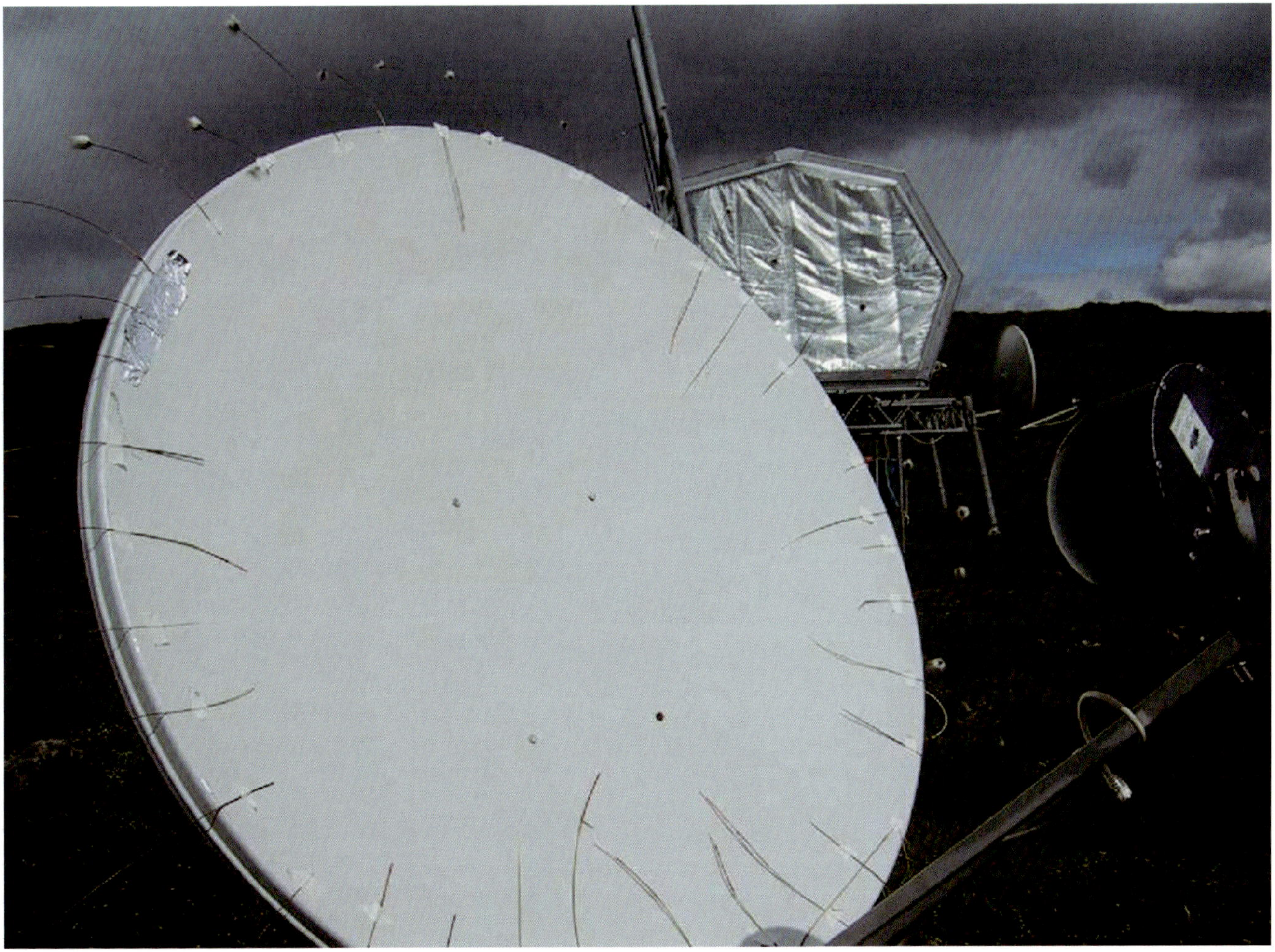

close as to where we were going to get where two F-15 fighter aircraft had crashed one wintry April night in 2001. Both pilots had been killed, probably instantly, though a search and recovery attempt was made that lasted weeks, hampered as it was by filthy weather.
My hands chilled while working on the

Intuitive Drawing
Helena Johard

ignition system of the fragile stick of paper, balsa and plastic that made up the rocket. Everything was getting soaked. It was a design of the camera mounted in the nosecone of the rocket that its switch was at the base of the nose, so some dismantling of the assembly had to take place prior to launch. With the

wet and all this meant huddling on my knees with my body shielding the fragile object while I ensured everything was still intact from the journey up the slope.
The rocket is fully prepped now so we slide it onto the thin steel rod that's mounted to a camera tripod. The camera is switched on, a picture

appears (thank God) and at the last possible moment I attach the ignition clips. Were we still receiving an image? Is it in the right position? Yes. Then let's go. 5-4-3-2-1 ignition. Dead. Adjust croc clips. Push the button again. No, nothing. I inspect the igniter after removing it from the rocket motor – it's gone,

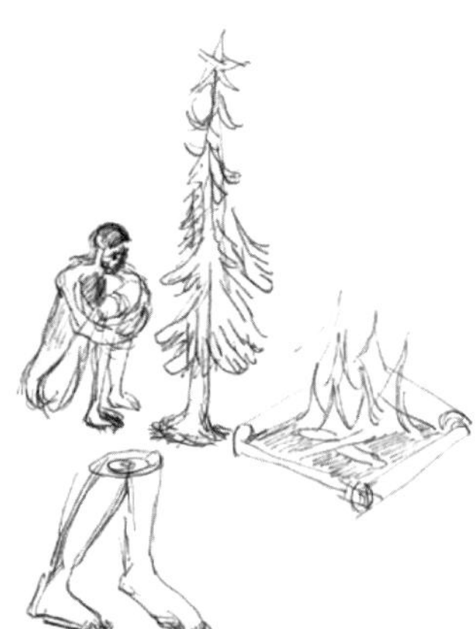

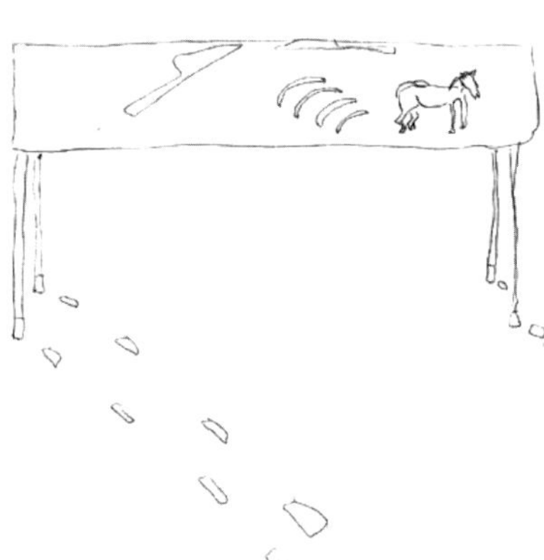

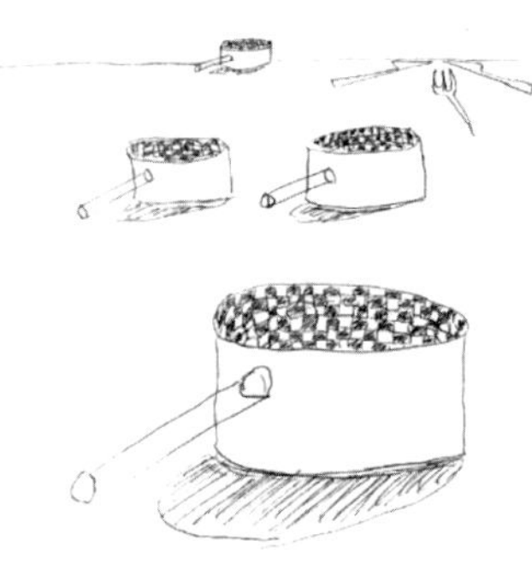

dead, burnt out, burning too slowly to ignite the black propellant it nestled beside. I suspect a dead or dying PP5 battery was the cause and exchange it for a fresh one.
Dan is getting jittery. He's worried the fine cable that feeds the all too important video signal to the land based DV camera will be getting water logged by the continual wetness we're engulfed with. I hurry but my hands are freezing and are losing their mobility. A fresh battery and igniter brings no further success. Dan covers the rocket with a plastic bag while I consider the options. I want to use a video camera battery to fire the charge as I've come to the conclusion that the cold of the hilltop is rendering the PP5's useless. Unfortunately I will have to destroy my hand held launcher to adapt it to use the video battery.
As this is only the first wild flight of the project I'm having difficulties deciding to do this especially when there is no guarantee it will work. With the

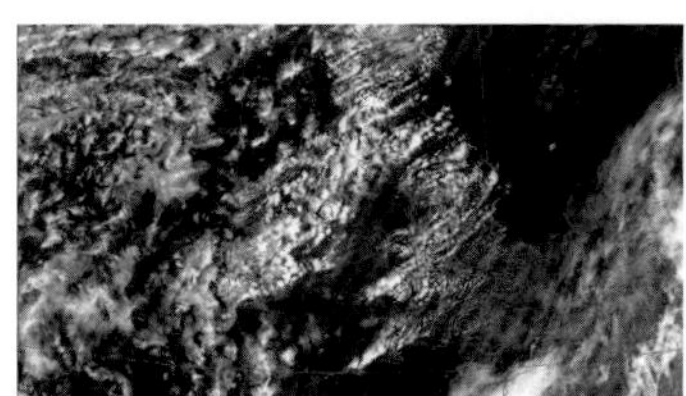

Intuitive Drawing
Helena Johard

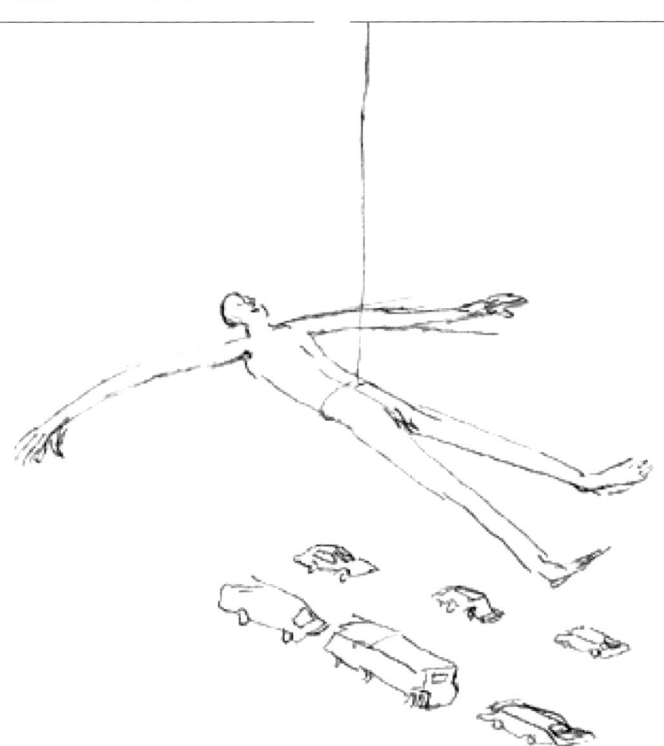

Over the last year I have been making drawings and videowork in parallel with biological research investigating receptor proteins in the nervous system of insects. My interests coincide theoretically in the paradox of how identity and perception of reality is both individual and communal. In the nervous system, the identity of a nerve-cell is ambiguously situated between being a discrete unit and being part of a large network of cell-to-cell communication. Our perception of reality and identity are explicitly defined by language based on social agreements, binding society together by exchange and cooperation. In parallel, a subjective, implicit and subconscious perception of reality exists opening up space for the unknown, a site for fear, curiosity and creativity. I believe the subjective side of our perception and processing of reality has a non-linear quality within social systems and is a necessity for generating mutations and change. The focus in my art practise is the space outside the borders of social constrictions where I use drawing and video as intuitive tools to non-verbally communicate with myself and others. In Makrolab I used a daily drawing routine to process my immediate environment and to record performative actions within this context. In this way I used non-linear research tools to operate within Makrolab where the outcome is a blend of my private life, interactions with crew and daily practicals in the bare landscape of Atholl estate.

Matthew Biederman

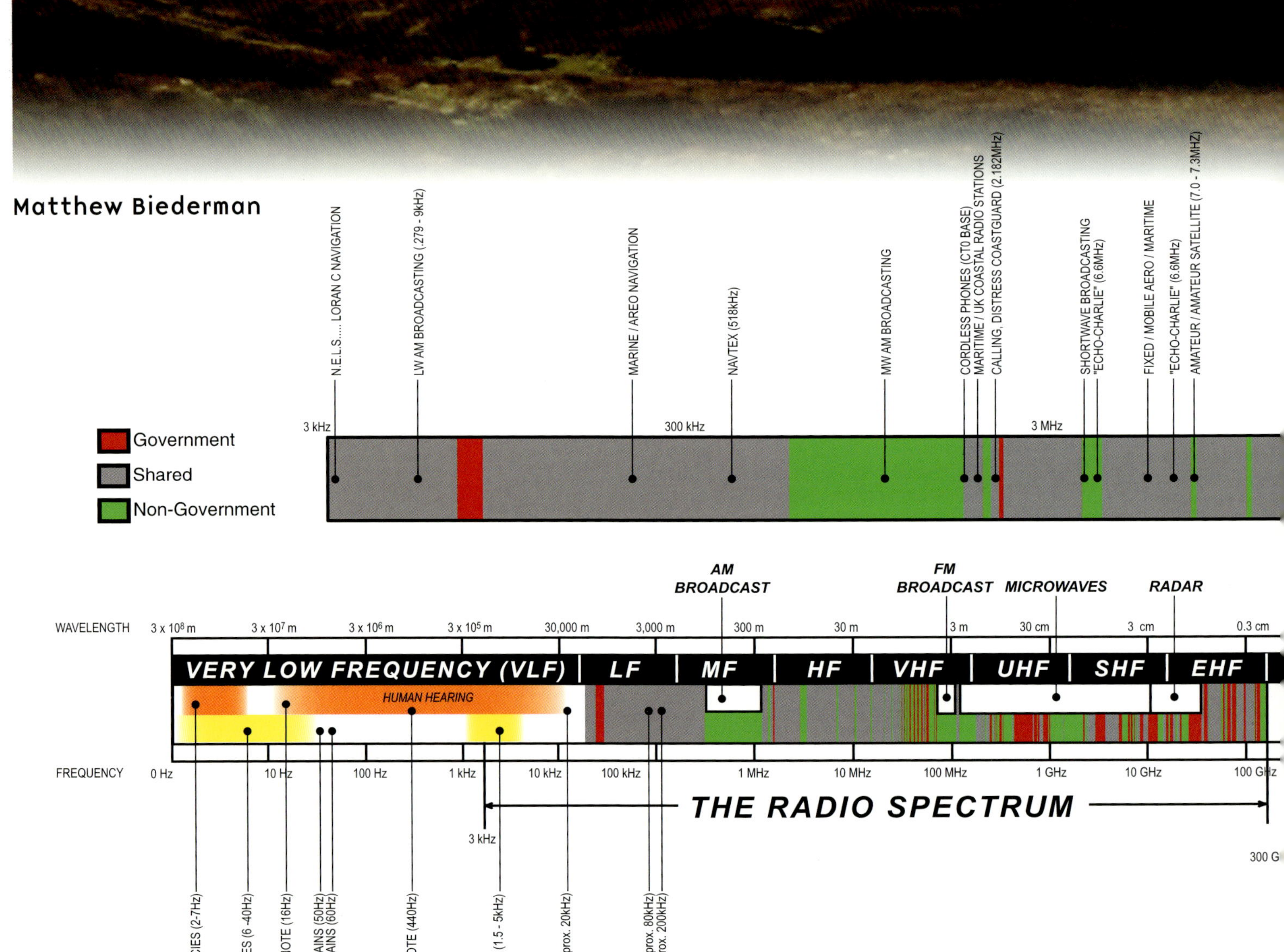

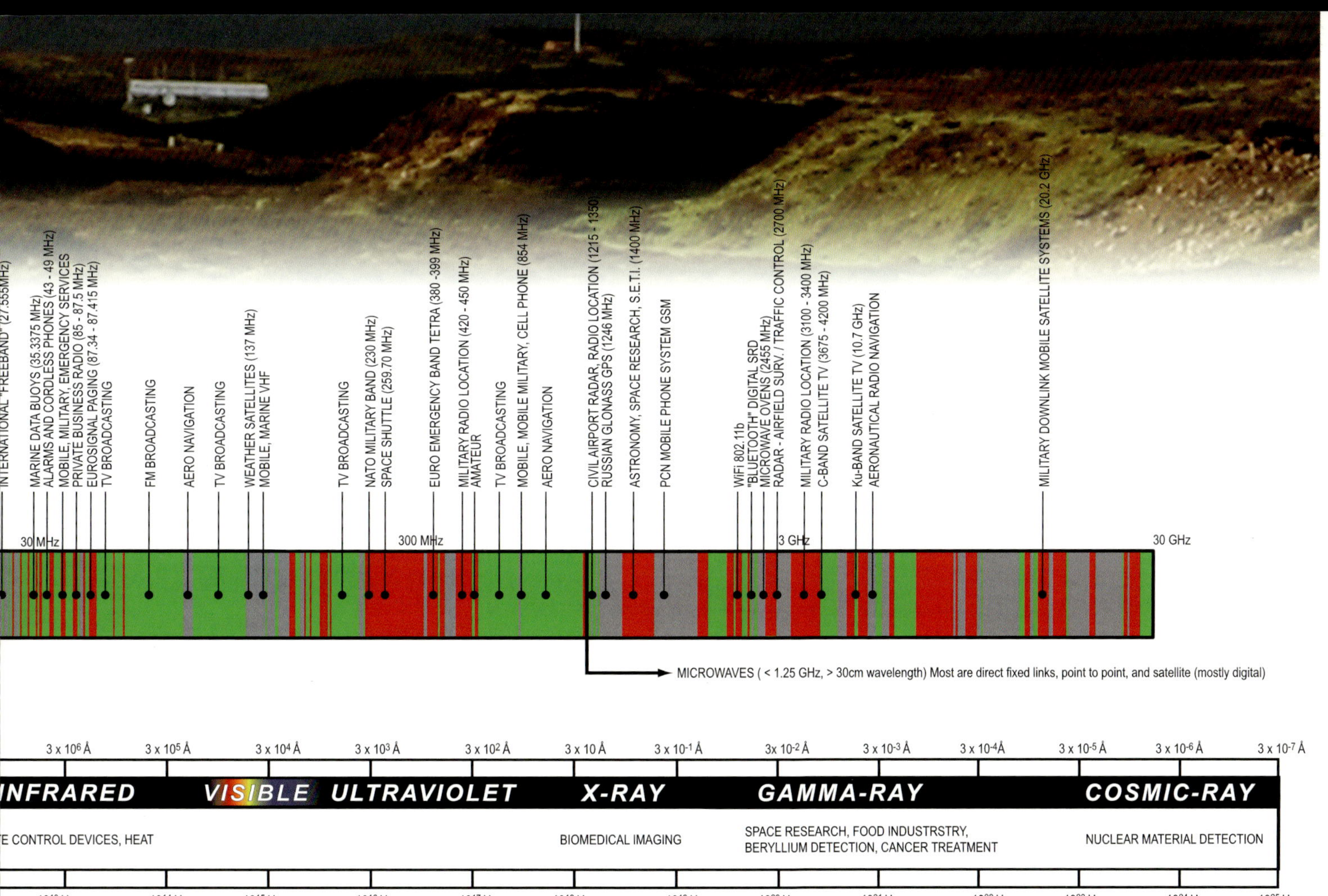

INTERNATIONAL "FREEBAND" (27.555MHz)
MARINE DATA BUOYS (35.3375 MHz)
ALARMS AND CORDLESS PHONES (43 - 49 MHz)
MOBILE, MILITARY, EMERGENCY SERVICES
PRIVATE BUSINESS RADIO (85 - 87.5 MHz)
EUROSIGNAL PAGING (87.34 - 87.415 MHz)
TV BROADCASTING
FM BROADCASTING
AERO NAVIGATION
TV BROADCASTING
WEATHER SATELLITES (137 MHz)
MOBILE, MARINE VHF
TV BROADCASTING
NATO MILITARY BAND (230 MHz)
SPACE SHUTTLE (259.70 MHz)
EURO EMERGENCY BAND TETRA (380 -399 MHz)
MILITARY RADIO LOCATION (420 - 450 MHz)
AMATEUR
TV BROADCASTING
MOBILE, MOBILE MILITARY, CELL PHONE (854 MHz)
AERO NAVIGATION
CIVIL AIRPORT RADAR, RADIO LOCATION (1215 - 1350)
RUSSIAN GLONASS GPS (1246 MHz)
ASTRONOMY, SPACE RESEARCH, S.E.T.I. (1400 MHz)
PCN MOBILE PHONE SYSTEM GSM
WiFi 802.11b
"BLUETOOTH" DIGITAL SRD
MICROWAVE OVENS (2455 MHz)
RADAR - AIRFIELD SURV. / TRAFFIC CONTROL (2700 MHz)
MILITARY RADIO LOCATION (3100 - 3400 MHz)
C-BAND SATELLITE TV (3675 - 4200 MHz)
Ku-BAND SATELLITE TV (10.7 GHz)
AERONAUTICAL RADIO NAVIGATION
MILITARY DOWNLINK MOBILE SATELLITE SYSTEMS (20.2 GHz)
30 MHz
300 MHz
3 GHz
30 GHz
MICROWAVES (< 1.25 GHz, > 30cm wavelength) Most are direct fixed links, point to point, and satellite (mostly digital)
3 x 10⁶ Å
3 x 10⁵ Å
3 x 10⁴ Å
3 x 10³ Å
3 x 10² Å
3 x 10 Å
3 x 10⁻¹ Å
3x 10⁻² Å
3 x 10⁻³ Å
3 x 10⁻⁴ Å
3 x 10⁻⁵ Å
3 x 10⁻⁶ Å
3 x 10⁻⁷ Å
INFRARED
VISIBLE
ULTRAVIOLET
X-RAY
GAMMA-RAY
COSMIC-RAY
E CONTROL DEVICES, HEAT
BIOMEDICAL IMAGING
SPACE RESEARCH, FOOD INDUSTRSTRY, BERYLLIUM DETECTION, CANCER TREATMENT
NUCLEAR MATERIAL DETECTION
10¹³ Hz
10¹⁴ Hz
10¹⁵ Hz
10¹⁶ Hz
10¹⁷ Hz
10¹⁸ Hz
10¹⁹ Hz
10²⁰ Hz
10²¹ Hz
10²² Hz
10²³ Hz
10²⁴ Hz
10²⁵ Hz

uncertainty I begin to see failure as something quite possible. There is only so long a cardboard rocket will withstand these elements before turning to mush and all the while its cable gets wetter and wetter until it doubles the mass the rocket must lift. Before we reach this point I make a discovery. I'm carrying a spare

minicamera battery that I've adapted to carry a PP5 clip and it fits my hand held launcher perfectly. 5 to 1 count and nothing! Shit. Forgot to attach ignition switch to rocket. Try again and the accelerating hiss of a big tyre going down fills the silent patch of hill we're on. I'm still looking at the ground, taken by surprise and expecting failure.

The rocket has vanished into the cloud and I hear Dan's throaty laugh "superb flight Milo".
It is. A perfect parabola and parachute deployment. The green of the twin chutes are quickly spotted down wind and down slope and I run, anxious to check no cabling has come loose while forgetting to look at the DV monitor

which would much quicker give me that info. A whisper of smoke vanishes in the wind. I barely have time to enjoy this moment as I unclip the rocket from its cable and charge back to the DV camera to check the results. It's a fantastic mixed success. The whole flight has been recorded, though with the mist the results show little of our site. It's

The Earthbound Satellite
Lisa Parks and Ursula Biemann

Experiments in Satellite Media Arts (ESMA) is a collaborative project produced at Makrolab in Scotland from June 17 - July 4, 2002 by Lisa Parks and Ursula Biemann. We spent two weeks at Makrolab downloading and manipulating satellite images, raw satellite television feeds, and electronic/digital sounds to generate a series of "orbital videos" that represent and comment upon contemporary global conditions. The project uses remote sensing satellite images and satellite television feeds to represent such issues as the war in Afghanistan, UN occupation of former Yugoslavia, conflicts in the Middle East, and immigration along the US-Mexico border. One of the goals of the ESMA project is to explore how media-makers might use satellite technologies as means of artistic and activist expression rather than as technologies of scientific observation, military monitoring, and meteorological forecasting. This series of videos is designed both to represent particular political conditions in the world and to explore the potentialities and limits of satellites as technologies of knowledge and representation.

We imagined our time in Makrolab as an 'orbital happening' and as an experience in 'remote sensing', which was aptly reinforced by Makrolab's own remote location in the Scottish highlands during summer 2002 and its access to the world through computer, satellite, and television technologies. We imagined Makrolab metaphorically as an earth-based satellite, and we used GPS to expose our 'location' by mapping our own migrations to, from and around Makrolab, and by downloading satellite images and downlinking satellite TV feeds while we were there. The result is a series of six 3-minute videos, each conceived as an orbit around the earth. Each 3 minute video is offered as a 'visual launch pad' for future artistic and activist experimentation with satellite, video, and computer technologies. We provide below the text of voiceovers from four of the videos.

ORBIT 1.0 MAKROLAB
Makrolab is like an earthbound satellite that passes from continent to continent. It senses, relays, exchanges, intercepts the noise and the silence.

Inside we monitored the orbital position

of the International Space Station as if we were monitoring ourselves.

The lab is a self-sustaining system that relies on a symbiosis of inside and outside, survivalism and high-technology, isolation and community.

This silver cocoon protects us from the elements outside, the same elements that generate our power on the inside. Makrolab runs on the energy of the wind and our bodies.

Laboring at lightspeed we lurk in the night ether. Signals fall to the earth, we capture them. They enter our capsule and become the domain of our experiments.

ORBIT 2.0 POSITIONING
In Scotland we connected with people nearby who use satellites on a daily basis. We visited the Dundee Satellite Receiving Station.

We discovered a very open environment and met technicians who use NOAA, Seastar, Meteosat and Terra satellites and make images available to the global public.

not important. The action has been carried out. We've launched a fragile rocket from a hostile mountaintop and returned the results safely to earth. We whoop with joy at having achieved this meaningful futile act of pilgrimage. We hastily pack up and plough on down to our next site, chuffed with the apparent success of our eccentric adventure. Its success in our own terms of course, as few other frequenters of this hill would understand that we climbed Ben Macdui to within 70m of the summit but didn't go there. It's a big day out and we weren't finished yet. Our next target lay 300m below us at Loch Etchachan. Downwards. It was early July and we were passing snowfields left over from a spring melt that never got this far. This was the Cairngorms, I reminded myself. It's big and it's bloody. Dan's dodgy knees were providing plenty of material for survivalist laughs even though we were both silently aware that our

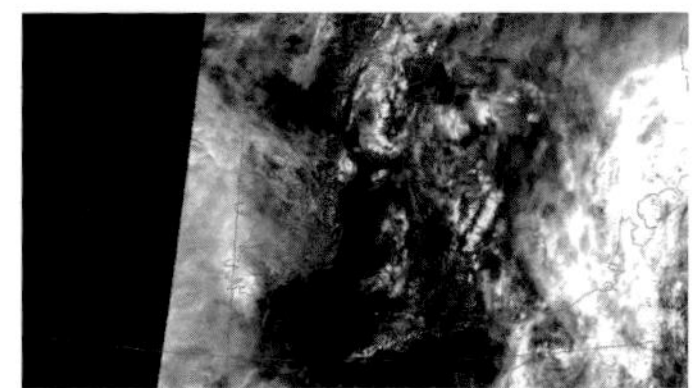

The station, which formed in 1978, operates with a medley of old and new technologies, analogue and digital, grounded and orbiting, monitors that measure time and map space.

We use Dundee satellite images in our experiments as terrains in which to map and measure our own positions at and around the Makrolab.

Using GPS we find ourselves in search of a position, a signal, a view. We sense, measure and map our environment to generate tracks,

We write on the earth by walking. We become movement signatures.

How can we position ourselves across these different surfaces, territories, earthly skins?

Satellite images can be layered and combined to illustrate the complexity of location and mobility, These are the shifting surfaces of global positioning, Cartographic stills that become kinetic fields.

ORBIT 3.0 FOOTPRINTING
Satellite dishes are scattered across the planet, receiving signals in various footprints.

When a satellite sends its signals, it leaves a trace on the earth.

A footprint is the geographic area in which a satellite's signals can be received.

A footprint is a domain of translation, where the encoding and decoding of culturally charged signals takes place.

A footprint is also a zone of contention. We scanned signals, focusing on the middle east, listening to their coverage of world events and we began to watch differently...seeing and hearing the signal splatter, the visual echoes... scrambled geographies... linguistic modulations... and political contradictions caught in our dish.

ORBIT 6.0 ORBITING
What does it mean to orbit?

Is it a technical process? A position in space? A state of mind?

We imagined our time in Makrolab/EXPERIMENT as an orbital happening, a collaboration unfolding on the periphery of civilization's centers.

While there we learned that satellites can function as technologies of isolation as much as they serve as machines of global integration.

To be in one's own orbit, as they say, is to turn inward while also remaining a little 'out there'.

But orbit can also refer to the cyclical and rhythmic relations that form between self and others, the self-patterning that also becomes global positioning.

Orbiting is about uplinking and downlinking, translation signals, making exchanges with others and positioning one's self.

position was remote and the hill was quiet that day.
We broke out of the clouds high on a steep shoulder that looked down at the loch. It seemed small, a mere pond but the height was fooling us. Sheer cliffs and steep banks surrounded it on all sides but one giving it an ominous feeling, and a healthy stream poured over a steep drop off that was our path back to the valley. As we descended we kept our eyes open for a good launching spot and it soon became clear from the shouts below that we weren't by ourselves in this otherwise lonely place. A green tunnel tent was stretched out on the soft moss on the flats that surrounded the expansive Corrie Lake. They were camping here, and may have been for some time as they had washing drying on the guy lines.

The story at this place was a benign one, fortunately. Two stranded walkers were stranded in November 2001 at a place North of where we were, caught in bad weather and disorientated in the dark. They were rescued by using the flashes on their cameras to attract attention. Mountain rescue saw them home safely. The story is a classic blend of ingenuity and luck and certainly befits an honorary rocket launch, especially as we are in the area.

The Earthbound Satellite
Lisa Parks and Ursula Biemann

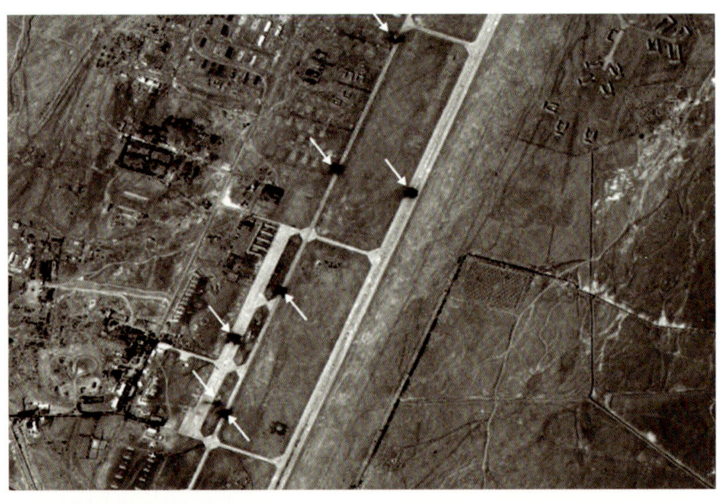

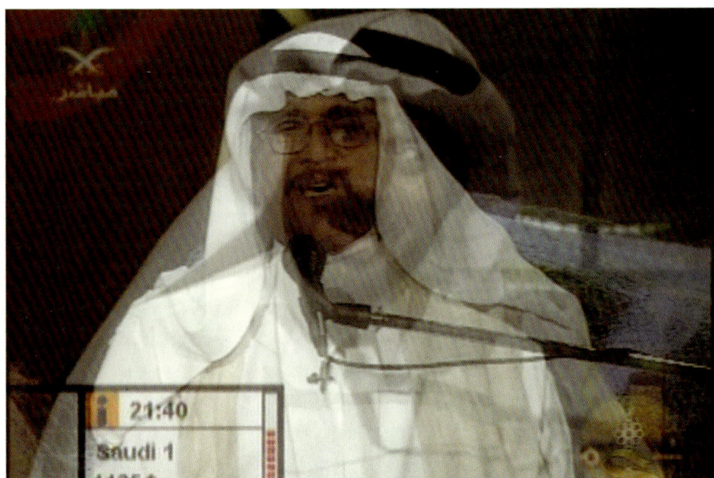

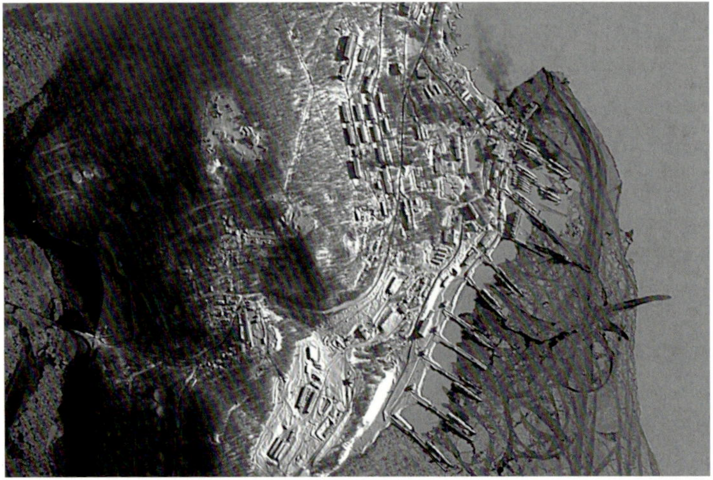

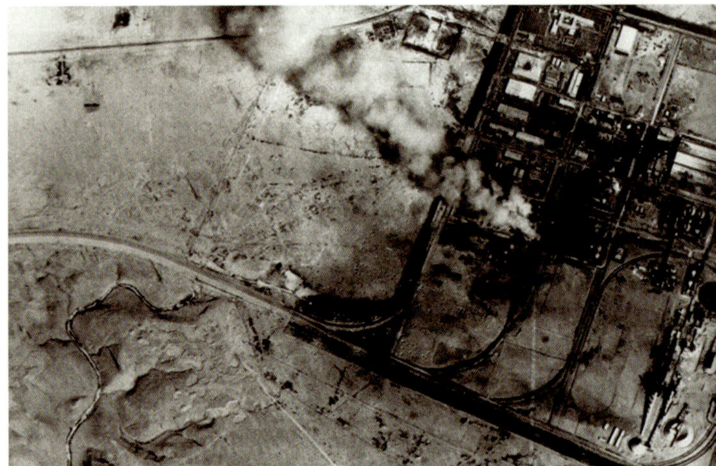

As its getting late we dispense with the more complicated paraphernalia of a take off and stick the launch rod in the soft ground. We move more quickly, falling into the roles that we practised back at the Makrolab and for real on top of the hill. The ignition system is connected, the video signal checked and even skipping the countdown I press the button. The damp silence of the mountain lake is momentarily broken by a sharp exhale. The exhaust gases of the rocket fall heavily to the ground, carpeting the area with a sluggish mist. Another perfect launch, higher than the last with hopefully a good view of the lake.

There is murmuring from the tent and the sound of a zip being pulled down. Dan and I are chuckling to ourselves as we run around collecting pieces and coiling cables. I'm concerned that I've lost a piece of fire proofed tissue. I know it will dissolve to nothing in this weather but I don't like leaving shit around in this rugged beauty. We're

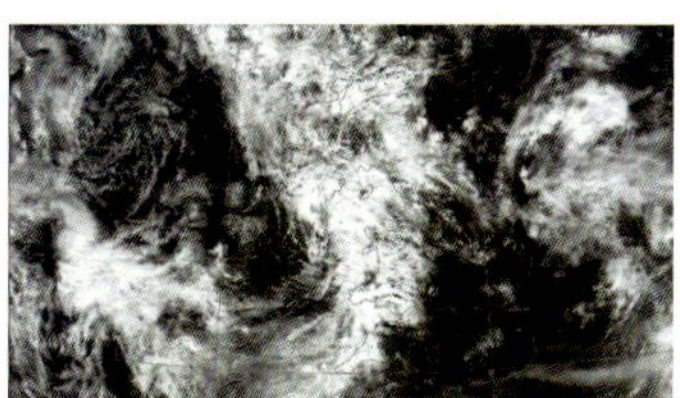

Impact of Grazing in Forest Regeneration
Tomasz Szymura

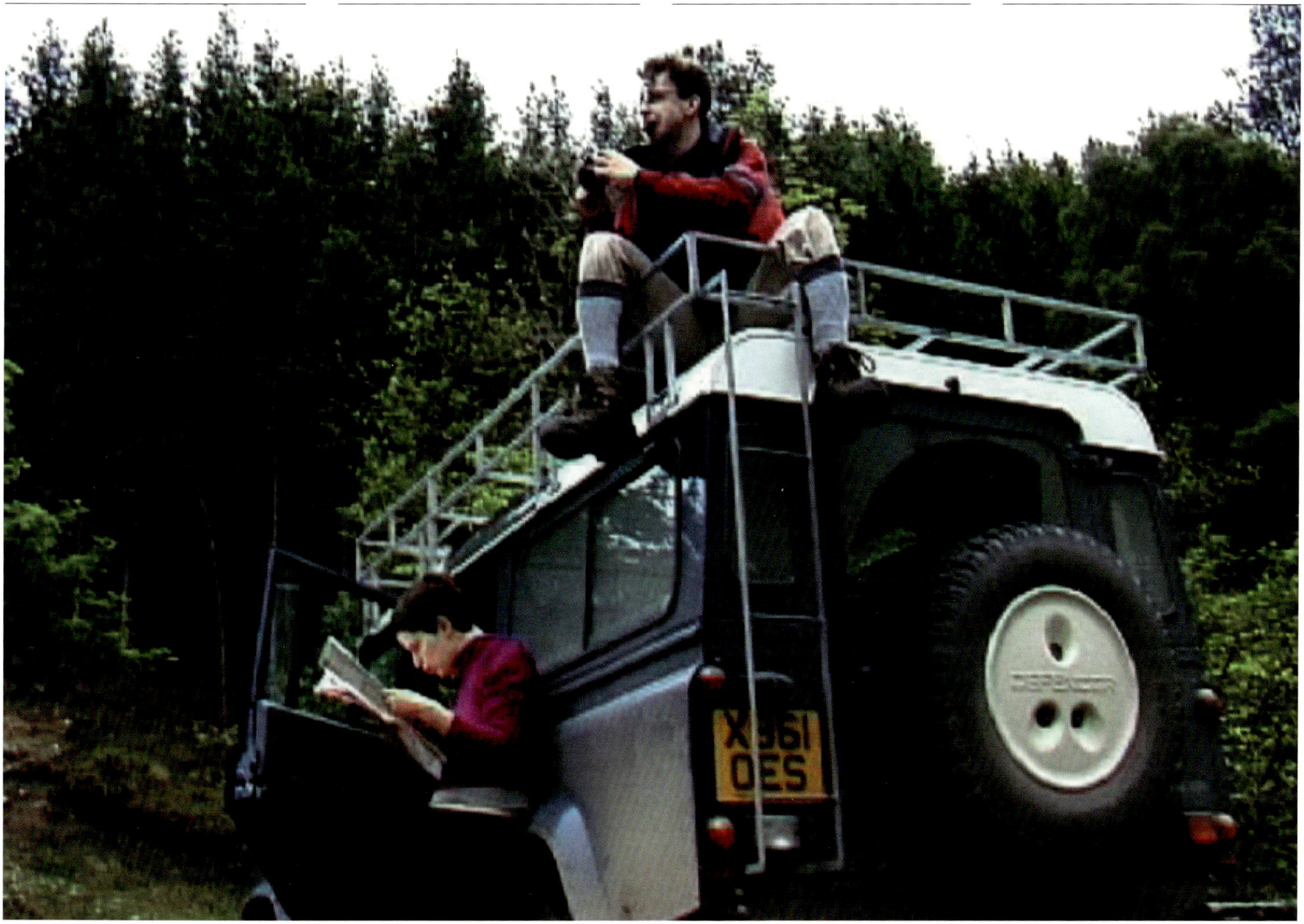

visitors and spies and I want to leave nothing here but impressions and take nothing but pictures.

We follow the stream homewards and rest at the Hutchinson's Memorial Hut for brews, celebrations and hilarity. The day had been a success so far. Two rocket launches in wild remote mountain territory. The first was the hardest as we were near the summit of one of the biggest mountains in Britain, total prep and launch time being over an hour and a half. The second showed us how smooth things could be. Total time – 20 minutes. Our journey back down the hill was protracted but pleasant, the downhill cycle from Derry Lodge a whooping joy in the longest evening sun of June. We were dog tired by the time we reached the Landrover at about 11.00pm. We had set off at 8.00am. Our journey back to the lab was almost an epic again on our discovery that the petrol was near gone. I hadn't been watching the gauge on the way up and Landrovers are thirsty beasts. Mountain gods smiled on us though and we came upon the only garage in the Grampians still open at 12.00 am, 5 minutes before the last staff went home. Near miss avoided and only a meandering drive in the dark left for us to cover. We crawled into the Lab at 1.30am, laughing.
Miles Chalcraft

Impact of grazing in forest regeneration
Tomasz Szymura

Restoration of the native woodland resource in Scotland is now a conservation priority as presented, for example in Habitat Action Plants (HAP). Research undertaken by Scottish Natural Heritage (SNH) has demonstrated that the distribution of new woodland can have a major impact on the value for biodiversity and conservation. The cheapest and the natural way of widespread of forest is their natural regeneration. Lack of regeneration in many upland woods in Scotland associated with grazing and overbrowsing by sheep and deer causes serious problems for their long term survival. The invertebrates, can affect vegetation changes. The best known effects are caused by browsing on young tress, shrubs and herbs, which alters both structure and composition and may retard woodland succesional development. Damage by twig browsing is an increasing problem in many European countries. The role of grazing frequently results in conflicts between foresters, landowners, hunters, nature conservationist, federal authorities and even tourists. The goal of my work is to assess the quality and quanttity effects of ungulates on natural forest regeneration.

METHOD

Research area: 140 yers old, human made pine stand in Glen Banawie Wood, near Blair Atholl (56° 47' 80.5'' N 3° 55'50.2'' E, altitude 330 m., British Grid reference number NO 823 694).
Established are two research plots each of area 120 m² (40 x 3 m.). The plots were similar concerning stands type, density of crown layer and ground vegetation, located close to each other, but one in open area (grazed) and second, in fencing area (ungrazed). The open area was penetrated mainly by deers, and occasionally by sheep.
In each research plot I counted number and height of seedlings of each seedling species, assesed density of crown layer and species stucture as well as density of ground vegetation layer.
Additionally I noted the vegetation species in which seedlings were growning.

RESULTS

The ground vegetation is composed mainly by bilberry Vaccinium (50%), Deschampsia (21%), heather Calluna vulgaris (14%) and mosses (10%); mean cover of this layer was 96% and dont differ significantly between plots. The mean density of crown layer was 25% and dont differ dignificantly between grazing and ungrazing plots.
On the plots I found the seedlings of following species: rowan (Sorbus aucuparia), scots pine (Pinus silvestris) and birch

(Betula pendula), the height varied from 0.2 to 1.5 m. (fig 1 and 2). In ungrazed area occured only litle rowan's seedlings, of which were damaged by browsing. The seedlings prefered disturbed microhabitats (e.g. uprooting mound) and pacthes covered by mooses. The seedlings avoided Deschampsia patches (fig 3).

DISCUSSION

The composition of ground vegetation (presence of weak by competitive bilbery and mosses) and density of crown layer (high access of light to ground layer) indicate conditions proper for reneowing of forest trees. In spite of existence of similar habitats and ground vegetation conditions, on grazed area the numbers of seedlings was more than seven times lower.
Additionally long-term grazing can increase the presence of wavy Hair grass (Deschampsia flexuosa) – species high competitive to seedlings.

CONCLUSIONS

Decreasing number of seedlings [consequence: inhibition or absence of regeneration of forest]
Decreasing number of seedlings species [consequence: in future possible decreasing of biodiversity of further forests]
Lower height of seedlings [consequence: lower competition ability of tree seedlings in relation to species better fit to grazing e.g. grasses]

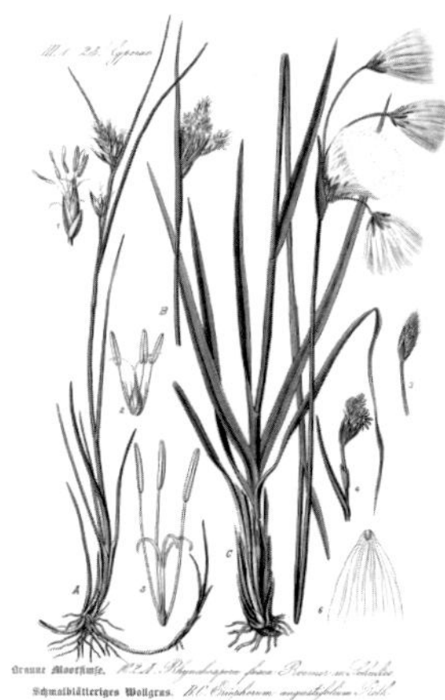

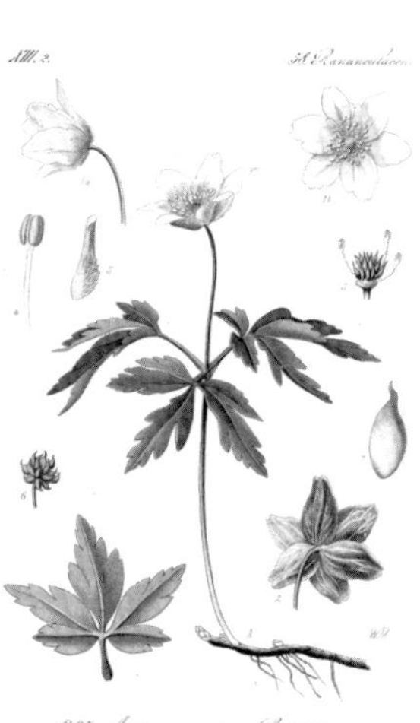

It rained almost the whole time. I woke up every morning and listened to the weather. The rain sounded different every morning depending on the wind, the type of the rain; big drops, small drops. Someone got up and made coffee and slowly other people made moves from their bunks and started occupying the workstation. The soundscape changed when someone turned on the television and satellite images from distant places appeared, accompanied by volume of exotic tunes and languages no one could understand. People connected over coffee and breakfast before disconnecting again, emerging into their own private spaces by linking up to the outside world of media information via satellites.
I think I have been realising more and more since I came here that the reason why I sort of feel out of place here is because I am out of place here.

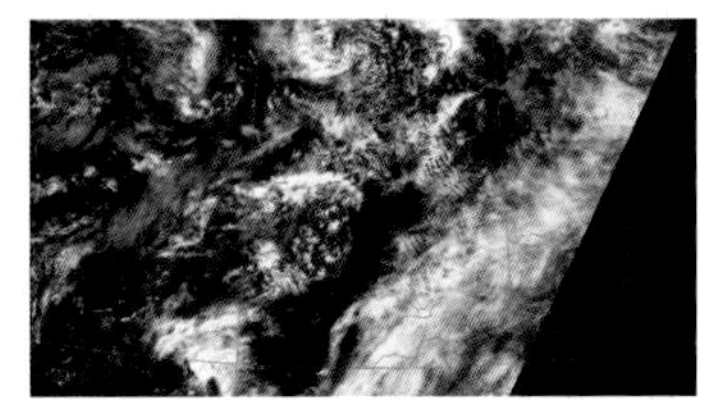

25 Hour Living
Ewen Chardronnet

Interview with the I-weather.org consortium who are working on the elaboration of an artificial climate based on the human biological clock.

"Like G.W.F. Hegel, we situate architecture at the lowest level of the world, in the midst of gravity and matter, beneath the variations of the climate and the passage of time, entangled in physical, chemical, biological and electromagnetic relations with the environment and our bodies."
Philippe Rahm and Jean-Gilles Décosterd

Marko Peljhan describes the "climatic sphere" of Makrolab with the concepts of insulation and isolation. Isolation through the choice of locations. Insulation because it is in contact with the world nonetheless, via technological means of communication. During each operation it is therefore necessary to take cognisance of the local "microclimate" (energy sources, etc.) and also to adjust to the variations of the "macroclimate" of the infosphere. Ultimately, Makrolab will be installed in the Antarctic as a permanent research base for artists and scientists. Reflecting on the prototype to be constructed for these extreme conditions, I wondered about the interior design structure for the new Makrolab, in the context of long-term missions. With a focus on artificial climate, based on the internal clock of i-weather.org. my questions were stimulated by the late night net-meeting organised by Stephen Kovats between the inhabitants of Makrolab and people living beneath the austral night in Antartica, taking melatonin.

Ewen Chardronnet: Could you describe i-weather.org?

Christophe Guignard: i-weather.org has set itself the goal of creating the world's first artificial climate to satisfy the metabolic and physiological requirements of a human being in an environment completely removed from all earthly influences: virtual reality, the disruption of the physiological clock that comes with air travel, and extraterrestrial trips and holidays. Accessible everywhere and to everybody thanks to the internet, i-weather.org makes it possible to live in a situation completely removed from natural locations by producing an artificial circadian rhythm synchronised to match the inner cycle of the human hormonal and endocrinal system.
In the absence of the natural terrestrial cycle of day and night, medical studies show that this inner cycle in fact lasts 25 hours, and that body temperature, the alternation between sleep and waking, and the accumulation and secretion of substances such as cortisone and oligopeptides, all depend on it. i-weather.org has therefore put together the first specifically human climate. It provides electronic architects, space agencies, digital artists and all other people creating projects outside the terrestrial cycle with a way to de-regulate the human circadian pacemaker.

For the moment i-weather.org operates solely on the basis of fluctuations in the rate of melatonin, which is influenced by variations in the intensity of light received by the retina and the skin. Henceforth, any electronic display connected to i-weather.org can act as a kind of personalised artificial sun, its light oscillating over a 25-hour period between a maximum intensity of 509 nm and a minimum intensity close to that of
...continued p42

This entry in my diary is the first sentence I wrote. I feel out of place because negotiating the body in different spaces is as much about an external bodily dialogues as well as internal one and the interaction of these two. A later diary entry provides a picture of the spaces provided:

It is interesting to think about the enclosed space inside the Makrolab itself. You are not only connected to the outside world through satellites and global media technology but also do you have connections to distant places through the people you are sharing this space with and who come from all over the world. How we connect somehow narrows all distances. And then you have the expansive space outside that extends itself to everywhere but still limits us, or encloses the whole situation.
I feel isolated I write again and again but this isolation takes on different forms. I feel isolated in the process of negotiating spaces with the people that share the Makrolab with me whilst in the process of finding my place amongst them. To escape I enter into my own private dialogue and one way of doing it is to is to move outside into the vast space of the Cairngorm mountains to extend the dialogue into different spaces with different pasts, presents and

[NOM]adic
Stephen Kovats

At nightfall the Makrolab [NOM]adic crew would set off on a journey beyond the station's physical realm to seek unknown interlopers – media transients – who themselves were ultimately disengaged from their habitual physical realms and identities. Each crew member would seek out individuals following network linkage paths irrespective of geographic locale. Often they would stumble into live conversations, or simply find individuals monitoring the interlopers who passed them by. Disjoined interlopers would then be brought together in server spaces where the crew, along with the newcomers would meet and exchange dialogue about movement, about perception of self within the anonymity of virtual space, about circadian rhythms, about the plausibility of zero gravity within telecommunications constructs, about their own practice within non-physical environments and the effects these have on their everyday sense of place.

The effect of such online linkups, randomly enabling the creation of instantaneous global communities, often resulted in the strengthening of urban environments devoid of buildings, as well as in the establishment of new social and private spaces. The telecommunications structures at hand worked to create a genuine fusion between the information space the crew were traversing and the fixed physical territories they normally occupy. By the removal of the architectonic structures we were inhabiting and focusing on telecommunications as such, the crew were able to actively study the nature of this communications space. Within the lab itself the crew, despite being mere touch-space apart, became both as removed from each other and as close as the wintering scientist at his isolated perch on the South Pole.

Makrolab became thus a universal media construct, its space entirely defined by the space of our communications beyond the lab's physical enclosure.

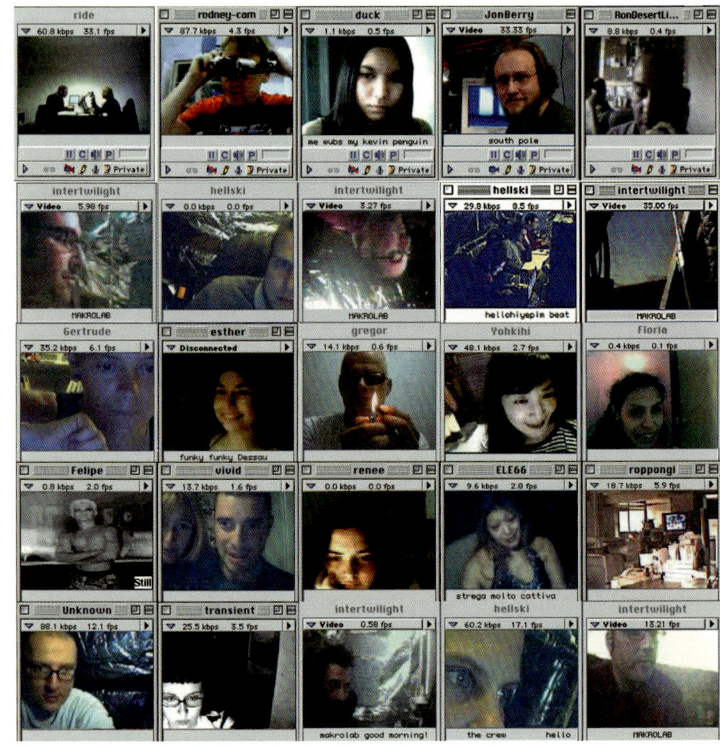

futures. These are localised spaces, not mediated through satellites but still the spaces that provide the location for the Makrolab which appears to be unconnected to it, an aluminum container from an invisible outside world. It is, nevertheless there and has emerged into the landscape, and at least temporarily,

it is a part of it and its histories. *The landscape was changing dramatically and I think that one of the reason why I always went further was curiosity. I wanted to see what was around the corner. It was wet and the wind had started blowing. I was wrapped up in my gear and regularly I felt like taking the hood*

down because I get tired of it – it blocks the connection to the landscape – you hear it differently. I was hungry and sat down to have a bite. I have never felt so on my own when I walk. There was no one around but me and the sheep and the mountains. Even though the farms I had passed were lived in spaces they

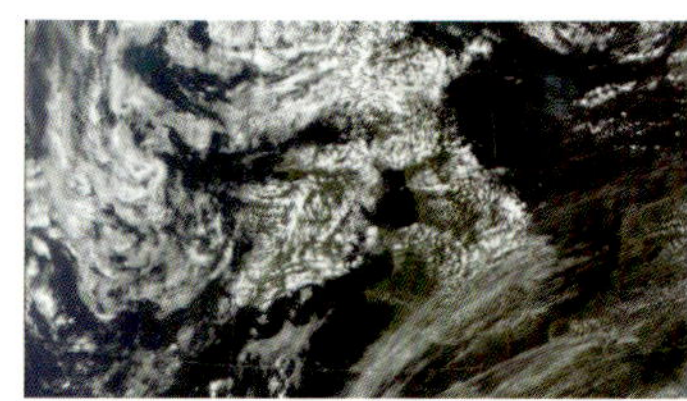

The Heliographer
Ewen Chardronnet

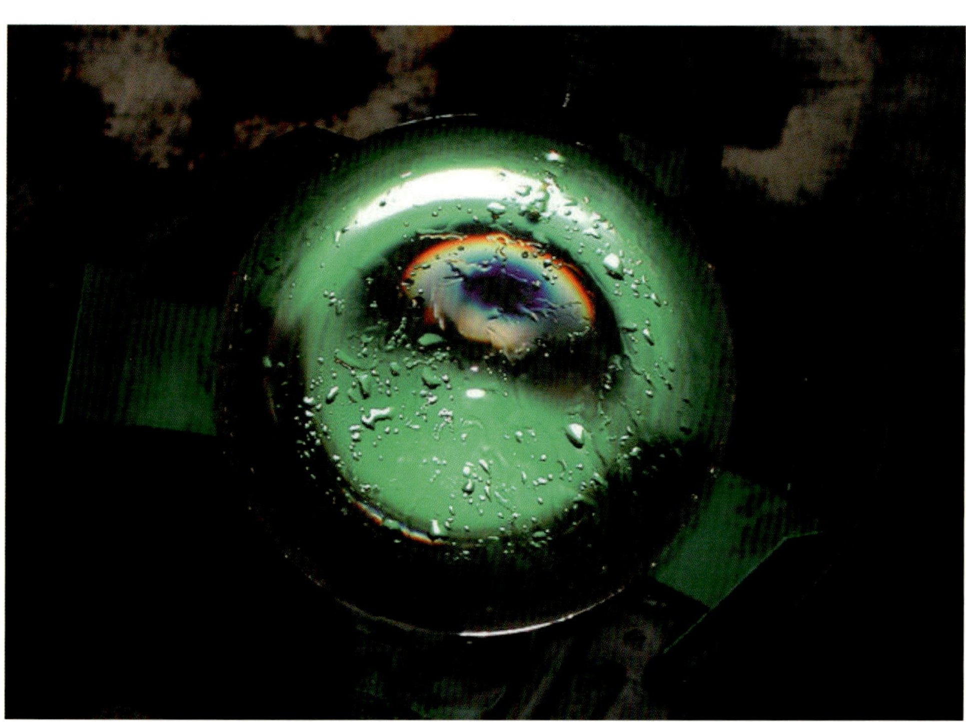

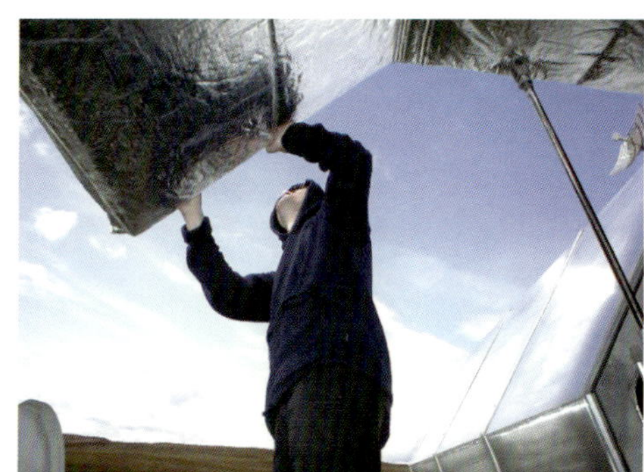

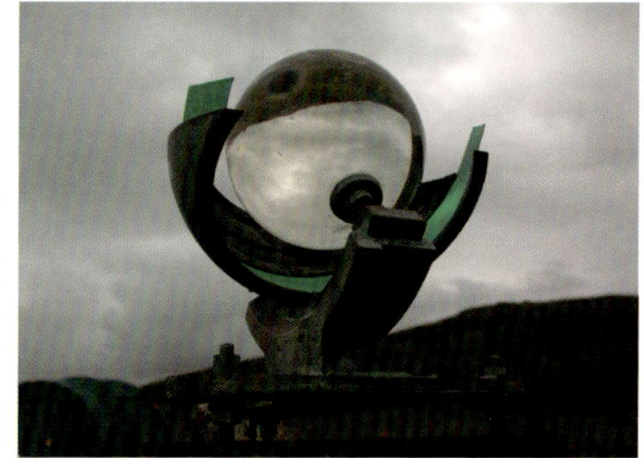

The heliographer is an instrument to take measures of numbers of hours of sun during the day. The sun rays burn a line on the paper through the glass. At Makrolab we used it for weather reports and weather sessions with children from the local nature club. (with the help of METEO FRANCE GUIPAVAS and the Sémaphore of the Isle of Batz, Brittany, France)

25 Hour Living
Ewen Chardronnet

42 ultra-violet (395 nm). This beta version will be improved on a continuous basis as and when scientific knowledge of biological rhythms increases.

EW: How does this artificial climate function?

CG: i-weather.org technology relies on a server that regularly delivers time synchronisation messages to all connected electronic devices. This permanent network connection ensures that all displays emit the same electromagnetic waves (between 395 and 509 nm) at the same time. The server is a generic multi-user server able to manage a 3D virtual space as well. It means that i-weather can also set the climate of an online 3D world using VRML technology, for example.

EW: Is it possible to be connected to i-weather.org or to use it in personal projects?

CG: As this technology is open source anyone can download it and transform their computer/pda/website/ virtual environment into an artificial i-weather source.

EC: Has some particular person served as a reference for the biological measurements? How can the system be adapted to any human body?

CG: The i-weather cycle is 25 hours, 07 minutes and 40 seconds long. This average cycle comes from medical studies of individuals isolated from any temporal information and from all environmental signals (rhythms of day/night, the seasons, etc.). For example, a French spelunker named Michel Siffre stayed inside a cave, totally cut off from the world, for over two months. His sleep/waking cycle ran for an average of 24 hours and 26 minutes (4 hours and 17 minutes of sleep for 20 hours and 09 minutes of waking). Other similar experiments have shown a cycle of over 25 hours. What emerges from these analyses is that the internal human clock is not based on 24 hours, but on a slightly longer cycle, hence the word "circadian," meaning "approximately one day."

In its current version, i-weather broadcasts the same intensity of light to all the individuals connected to the system. The system, while closer to the

internal rhythm of each person, is not yet personalised. It is nonetheless possible to imagine a later individual version, based on a personal medical analysis of the internal clock and the circadian rhythm. Supposing a range of +/- 50 minutes on either side of the average i-weather time, all of humanity would then be distributed into some one hundred parallel "personal" cycles, creating distinctions/comparisons between individuals which would no longer be based on notions of nationality or culture or proximity, but on their internal biological rhythm.

EC: The internal clock is 25 hours long? Are there rational (or irrational) explanations for that?

CG: Maybe a slowdown in the earth's rotation since the appearance, millions of years ago, of the TIM and PER (timeless and period) proteins that regulate the internal clocks of living organisms...

Phillippe Rahm: Paul Virilio said that daylight, after being the contrast between day and night, then the trembling light of the candle, and then finally the endless light of electricity, is but in an absence of land. This is slightly different then the erasure of the horizon line - a thick fog between the sky and the ground merging the stratosphere with the stratasphere. The area has multiple Arctic enthusiasts. In Pitlochry we spent part of the day at Glacier Books talking with the parents of C., the man who owns all the books. He has a massive collection of Arctic, Antarctic and mountain adventure stories, including an original newspaper clipping from the day before Scott's last day – an update on his expedition before it was known that it would be his last. We are trying to track down D. M., a failed Arctic adventure explorer nearby. He used an 02 phone on his expedition instead of Iridium. Seems to make for good deep long sleep here – cocooned in silver and constant repetition of rain on roof. All days start to blend into one so I have no idea what the number of the date is, but it must be in the teens of June. ...continued p52

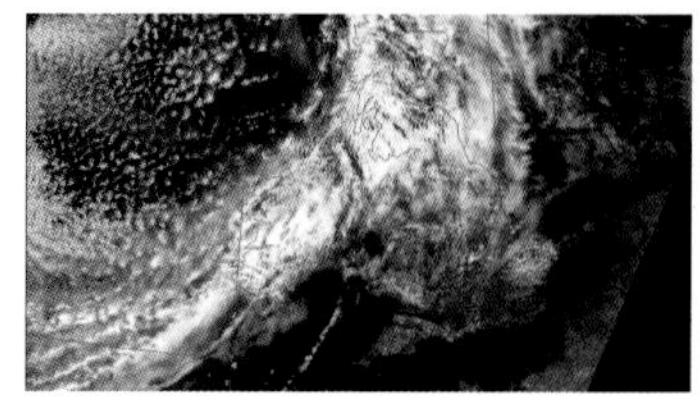

25 Hour Living
Ewen Chardronnet

now the light of computer screens, of instantaneous connections that can bring the light of the day in the midst of night, capturing daylight on the other side of the planet with web-cams. We are no longer in an astronomical relation with space that is already altered by electric light. With that project we criticised the idea that virtual worlds are virtual, and we accepted the materiality of virtuality. Our aim was to displace the architecture of mechanics, of gravitation, to shift it towards the electromagnetics which is constructed in the exchange between the screen's radiation and the retina of a networked world.

EC: What is the role of i-weather in your architectural approach?

PR: It's a very important project that brings the new technologies into relation with the organic. Anna Wirz-Justice writes in our book:
'If we examine current neurobiological and physiological phenomena, then we could bring i-weather into our rooms. In a "24/24" society, functioning and working in an artificial environment where day and night no longer have their primordial impact (even if the biological clock keeps ticking), a disordered, off-rhythm light-signal forms part of the sociophysiological malaise. Where is the rosy-fingered dawn signalling the hour of awakening, the midday sun, where are the passing clouds, the trembling leaves, the slow fall of dusk signalling nocturnal rest? Logical correction, amidst an artificial world, is the simulation of atmospheric conditions on a computer screen, the virtual becoming real, the absent outer world now reaching into the office and home with a dynamic interior architecture of shadow and light.'

EC: Do you plan to construct a prototypical living space where people could experience living with new contingencies (no natural light, absence of the day-night cycle, etc.), thanks to electronic solutions?

PR: The wintertime house that we are constructing in France this year for the French artist Fabrice Hybert includes a climactic disorder as architecture. We displace a Tahitian climate into the heart of winter in Vendée, with all its luminous and chemical characteristics, through the intensity and wavelengths of the light, through the odour and quality of the air.

See the following sites for the latest uses of I-weather and the work of architects Christophe Guignard and Phillipp Rahm

www.electroscape.org,
www.fabric.ch
www.fabric.ch/noosynaptic,
www.low-architecture.com

Time-painting has abandoned the indeterminacy of words and now possesses an exact unit of measurement.
Those who think they can ignore the pure Laws of Time and still make correct judgments will seem like the old tyrant who had the ocean whipped because it destroyed his ships.

They would do better to study the laws of navigation.
First I discovered the characteristic reversibility of events after 3^5 days, 243 days.
Then I continued to increase the powers and extents of the time periods I have discovered, and began to apply them to the past of humanity.

That past suddenly became transparently clear; the simple law of time suddenly illuminated it in its entirety.
I understood then that time was structured in powers of two and three, the lowest possible even and odd numbers.

I understood that the true nature of time consists in the recurrent multiplication of itself by twos and threes, and when I recalled the old Slavic belief in the powers of 'odd and even' I decided that wisdom was indeed a tree that grows from a seed. The superstition is all in the quotation marks.

KRK
Marko Peljhan

It was a sunny late winter day of 1994, the location the island of Krk, Adriatic Sea, Croatia. The 'Mjesec' (Moon) landscape above Baška. It is us, the inventors/explorers of the new sensibilities, children of number 317, walking high up above the sea, glistening in the sun and deeper blue than ever. The bay is far below. To the south Goli Otok, the barren landscape of this island with its recent horrific past of a high security prison and a genuine Yugoslav Gulag in the 50's and early 60's. Memories of the stories we have read about extensively during the evolutionary 80's, growing up. Deconstructing states. Projecting visions. To the east the Velebit mountains. A spectacular sight. Monumental. Barren. Cold. Silently majestic. Behind them occupied Lika and further East Udbina and Bihač. War. Me, Ivana and Ivan. This is a beautiful day. For the last week we have been discovering the secrets of dead cities, the flavours of local herbs, the Čaj za Mir (Tea for Peace), discussing what comes next, if this war will rage on. If our friends will die, disappear and whole city populations shift and cease to exist. What if this heavy winter silence doubles in weight during the summer and pulls everything down? What is next for us, the creators of the landscapes of the future?

We have been discussing what the theatre of the future should look like. What it should be. How to start living outside the three axes of Euclid and start understanding the laws of the fourth, the axis of time, so much revered by Velimir Khlebnikov. The language-sorcerer, the author of Ladomir, the discoverer of the Laws of Time, the inventor of the Tables of Destiny. Are we witness to the new battle of Tshushima, are we just being thrown around by the constructed history or is this is all just a learning situation? For the future. As we sit high above the sea, we hear thunderous noise coming from the east, but the sky is blue. There is a barely audible rhythm. The maddening powers at work. The towers of war. The battles of our lives. Not far away, death and destruction. High above the lonely combat air patrol, two small contrails. Lower and to the north, one of the Zagreb-Brindisi relief flights. A turboprop. Probably Spanish. Maybe. I wish I had my VHF transceiver with me. What exactly is going on? The visible and the invisible merge into an extensive landscape, the past and the future converge, the machines of construction and destruction working in unison. There is no forest, but the fate is ever present in these stones. We start talking about survival. Survival of the constructive,

inventive, exploring forces. Survival of performative systems during the deconstruction of society. I see stages move and walk by themselves, armoured and autonomous. Ivana laughs. As always. She constructs 'Litening' second skins . Stealing the sight of many, with a lightness of a thousand winds. But first I talk about the landscape of Ladomir. Right here, on the EarthMoon of Krk. People wrapped in survival cocoons, sleeping. Other people visiting them. They are silently talking to each other. A stage appears on the horizon and walks slowly forth. On it the sailors of Ladomir work the spinnaker of thought. Large sails propel it forward, a complex mechanism allows its legs to lift and twist. There are no metal noises. The materials are new and unknown. It does have legs and it looks like an insect. It has the functionality and energy balance of a bee and the armour of an Armageddon cockroach. I will discuss this with Jurij. I have to talk to him back home. What would the people do? will be his first question. I am quite sure about that. Understand and survive would be my first answer. By, for and on themselves. Operate and keep the legged drifter working, functioning. They will connect themselves to the satellites, they will roam the globe. They will discover its deep laws.

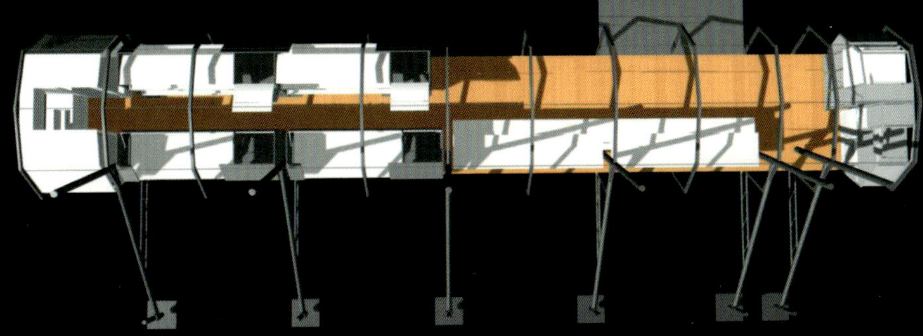

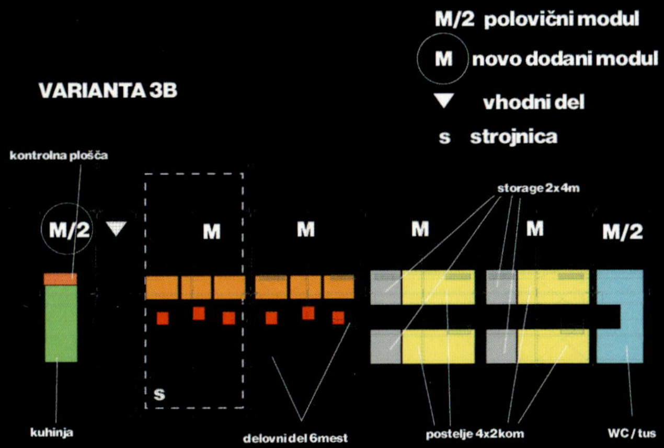

popravek variante predvideva 8 lezišč v spalnem delu, ki je lahko fizično ločen
od delovnega s pomično steno in 6 udobnih delovnih mest
hidroponične enote so v tem primeru v delovnem modulu za hrbtom posadke

Makrolab mark IIex architecture, 2003
Aljaž Lavric, Matevž Francic

Makrolab Architecture Team:
Matevž Francic
Aljaž Lavric
Marko Peljhan

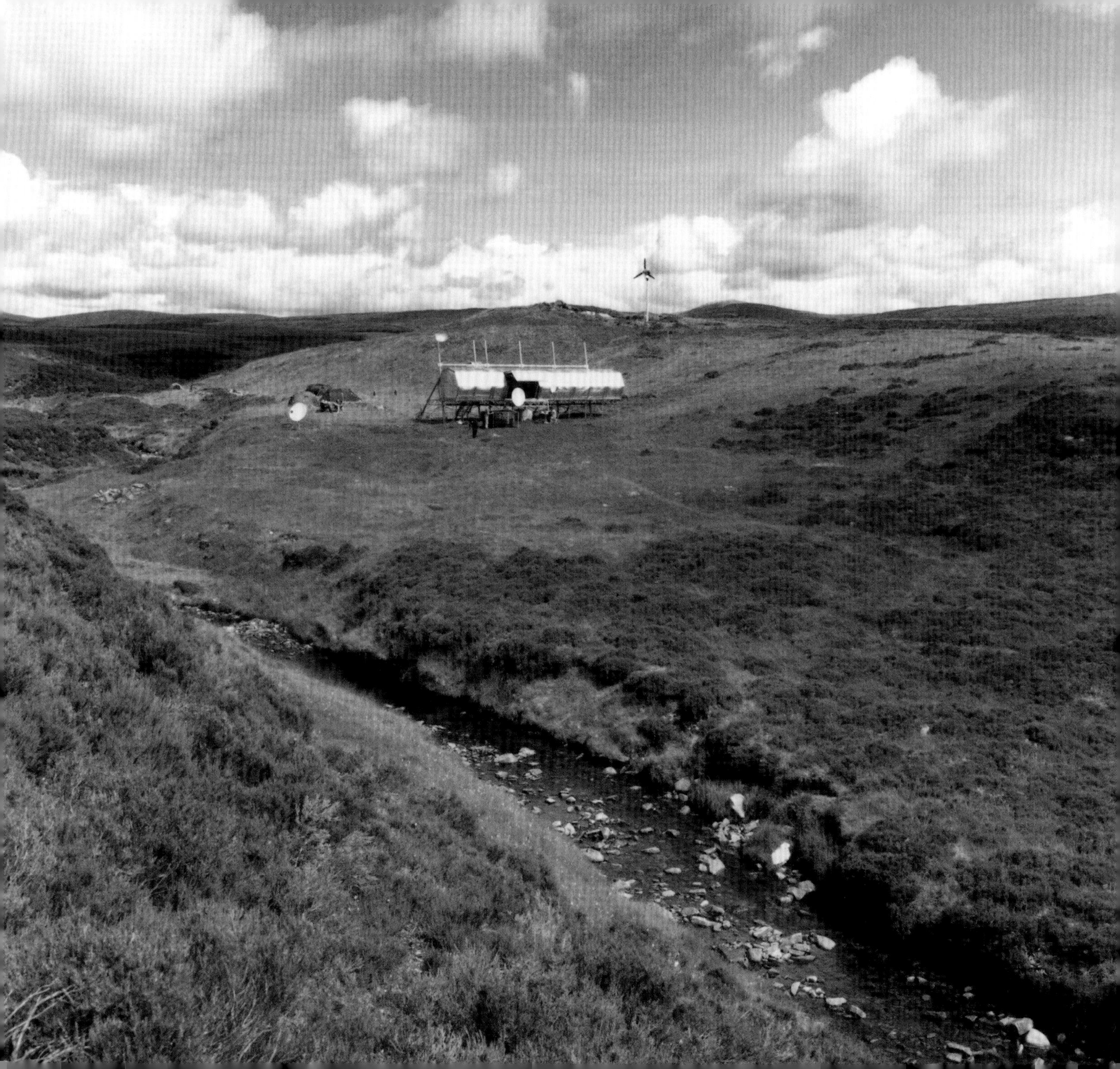

TELECOMMUNICATIONS

- SATCOM MAPPING AND REFLECTION
- BROADCAST SATCOM MAPPING AND REFLECTION
- HF MAPPING AND REFLECTION
- VHF/UHF MAPPING AND REFLECTION
- INSULAR TECHNOLOGIES NETWORK
- PUBLIC KEY CRYPTOGRAPHY DEVELOPMENT
- NETWORKS MAPPING AND TOPOLOGIES
- ATV TECHNOLOGY DEVELOPMENT
- WIRELESS IP MESH DEVELOPMENT
- IP/SEC DEVELOPMENT
- OPEN SOURCE INDEPENDENT SATCOM DEVELOPMENT
- REMOTE SENSING DATA ACQUISITION

MIGRATIONS

- BIRD MIGRATION PATTERNS AND NAVIGA
- CAPITAL MIGRATION MAPPING AND REFLE
- HUMAN ECONOMIC MIGRATIONS MAPPIN
- HUMAN LEISURE MIGRATIONS MAPPING A
- COMPREHENSIVE ECOLOGICAL IMPACT OF
- COMPOSITE MIGRATION INTERRELATION A
- COMPOSITE PLANETARY MIGRATIONS MA
- DOPPLER MIGRATION OBSERVATIONS AND
- HUMAN SEASONAL MIGRATIONS MAPPIN
- HUMAN ORIENTATION AND NAVIGATION C

COMPOSITE THREE FIELD ALGORITHM RESEARCH

MAKROLAB NETWORK CENTRIC NARRATIVE SYSTEMS

INSULATION / ISOLATION STRATEGY RESEARCH

CLOSED ECOLOGIES RESEARCH

NETWORK CENTRIC IDENTITY RESEARCH

ENERGY PRODUCTION, STORAGE, CONTAINMENT AND DISTRIBUTION SYSTEMS

1994
- MJESEC (KRK ISLAND)
- CONCEPTUAL BASE

1995
- ENGINEERING
- BASIC ARCHITECTURE PLANS

1996
- CONCEPT FINALISATION
- PREPRODUCTION ACTIVITIES
- INITIAL PRODUCTION ELEMENTS

1997
- PRODUCTION
- FIRST PROTOTYPE SETUP – May
- FIRST OPERATIONAL SETUP – documenta X
- MAKROLAB mark I OPERATIONS: June-September

1998
- ARCHIVAL WORK
- FIRST OVERHAUL
- MAKROLAB mark II DEFINITION
- mark II ENGINEERING PLANS

1999
- MAKROLAB mark II CAMPALTO CAMPAIGN
- PRODUCTION DEFINITION AND TIME PLAN
- PRODUCTION OF SECOND PROTOTYPE
- SECOND PROTOTYPE TESTING – December
- INSULAR TECHNOLOGIES SYMPOSIUM
- CONTAINERIZATION AND SHIPPING

2000
- SECOND OPERATIONAL SETUP – ROTTNEST ISLAND/WADJEMUP AUSTRALIA
- MAKROLAB mark II OPERATIONS: January-May
- INSULAR TECHNOLOGIES TEST: May
- TEST SETUP – VELIKI KRAS
- SECOND OVERHAUL

2001
- MAKROLAB mark III and IV ENGINEERING PLANS
- mark III and IV MODIFICATIONS PLANNING
- WIND ENERGY SYSTEM TESTBED
- MEDIUM TEMPERATURE EVALUATION TESTING
- TRANSHUB SPINOFF PROJECT DEVELOPEMENT
- TRANSHUB 01 PREPRODUCTION ACTIVITIES
- TRANSHUB 01 PRODUCTION

2002
- TRANSHUB 01 MU01PS MOBILATORIJ LAUNCH AND DELIVERY
- MAKROLAB mark III-IV PROJECT TERMINATION
- MAKROLAB mark IIx DETERMINATION
- MAKROLAB mark IIx SETUP PLANNING AND TESTING
- MAKROLAB mark IIx THIRD OPERATIONAL SETUP – Atholl Estates
- MAKROLAB mark IIx OPERATIONS: May-July
- ARCHIVAL WORK
- MAKROLAB mark V DEFINITION

2003
- ATHOLL ESTATES OPERATIONS/EMM PRESENTATION: Generali Foundation
- MAKROLAB COMM ENVIRONMENT SOFTWARE AND HARDWARE DETERMIN
- January-June COMM ENVIRONMENT SOFTWARE AND HARDWARE PRODUCT
- MAKROLAB mark V ENGINEERING
- MAKROLAB mark IIex MODIFICATION START: February
- MAKROLAB mark IIex COMPREHENSIVE ENERGY SUITE TEST: May
- MAKROLAB mark IIex INTEGRATION AND TESTING: April-May
- CONTAINERIZATION AND SHIPPING
- VENICE LAND COMM ENVIRONMENT SETUP
- MAKROLAB mark IIex FOURTH OPERATIONAL SETUP: Venice Biennale
- MAKROLAB mark IIex CAMPALTO ISLAND OPERATIONS: June-August
- MAKROLAB mark IIex NETWORK OPERATIONS: June-November

KRK
Marko Peljhan

★ Methods for the augmentation of maximum sensory awareness and sensory connection will be used throughout the work.

Ladomir-фактура is not only a work of art (with the limitations of that term), but a progressive activity in time, based on the belief that ritualisation of utopian conditions and forms and their projection in real space/time leads to concrete social evolution in the intermediate environment. This can then overcome the ever-actual discontinuity between the categories of art and natural, social and spiritual sciences and in turn converge in a wider definition, an optimal landscape of free creativity and integral individuality. The work is being developed in three stages:

★ The first stage consists of the engineering and projecting process (structure planning, construction of instruments and gears, construction planning, artistic material planning, historical research, programming)
★ The second stage is the particular materialisation of these processes using and taking advantage of different media, (performance, lectures, presentations, data media, publications, video) with the purpose of establishing a dialogue with a wider context.
★ The third stage is the materialisation of the Ladomir-фактура modular autonomous constructions and environments in nature, with open communication lines and memorisation and reflection modules. With it, the mapping of LADOMIR will begin in real space/time and the observation and evolution of the science of the individual will take place.

This was 1994 and eight years later, we have spent a little bit more than two months in the Makrolab markIIe, the third version of the Ladomir-фактура modular environment and construction. E standing for extended systems, although this time the extension did not go as far as we wished. But connected we were. Orbital jockeys, working at least three satellites at a time, landscape explorers, discovering the time-embedded secrets of the Atholl Estates and the Highlands, ionospheric divers, powering up the receivers and translating high frequency noise into visible modulation patterns, for the world to play with and understand. What we just barely understood ourselves. Lisa and Ursula frantically worked on their Brechtian orbital learning pieces. Brian came to visit for a few days, appropriately for the times, with a Geiger counter. Sometimes he reminds me of the Watchmen. The end is nigh... He brought Echelon into our lives in 1996. Myself, I have sailed into the seas of zero-point and Podkletnov and when Adam came up with the Van Eck works and the Phd thesis about them everything seemed very, but very normal. We have learned to navigate by now. Germany, Australia and Slovenia have proven perfect planes in this plan for the future. Our language has developed, our orientation has sharpened. Engineers of the new era. Matevž and Aljaž. And the hands and ingenuity of Jože and his colleagues. I have started to dream about automatic data logging and active sensors. As in the initial plan. And now we have them. We will start gathering the building blocks of the language of the new equation. Five more years of this project and this vision. We already treat the lake as the soup of life. It is time to go to work, as Velimir the First would say, Presidents of Planet Earth. The barren landscapes of the first EarthMoon are waiting and the new building is being shaped. We shall provide data for its perfect alignment. It will be armoured, autonomous and insulated. No energy will be wasted, no heat will escape. And it will talk with the planetary expanse.
(2003)

Once I had uncovered the significance for time of odd and even, I had the sensation of holding in my hands a mousetrap in which aboriginal Fate quivered like a terrified little animal. The equations of time resemble a tree, simple as a treetrunk in their bases, and slender and complexly alive in the branches of their powers, where the brain and living soul of the equations are concentrated; they seem to be the reverse of equations of space, where the enormous number of the base is crowned by one, two or three, but never anything further.
These were, I decided, two opposite movements within a single stretch of calculation.

Velimir Khlebnikov
(1922)

KRK
Marko Peljhan

They will be creators from all directions, brought on the platform by different winds. Scientists and artists. Discovering the laws of time. Of communication. Of the electromagnetic flux. Of the navigation of whales, birds and people. They will measure and calculate the dynamics of thunder and cells. They will equate and understand. The final equation and law. They will sail far away. At incredible speeds. And the world will become their stage. There is a little silence then. And Ivana laughs. And we still hear the explosions. And real is more real than real. When we walk down, I start to think about the perfect plan. The map. I decide I will write the first text for this project for the future. Here it is.

SCIENCE OF THE INDIVIDUAL — MAPPING OF LADOMIR

The redefinition of social and individual terms and the subsequent materialisation of their redefined status in new evolutionary conditions, demands appropriate physical, psychic and material preparation.
PROJEKT ATOL tries to enable the creative communication of individual forces to converge into a scientific/psychic entity that would in its last stage result in the creation of an insulated/isolated environment — space/time.
Insulation/Isolation is understood as a vehicle to achieve independence from and reflection of the actual entropic social conditions. The environment will serve as a development surface for the further formation of new creative, social, spiritual and economic relations, based solely on integral individuality.
Ladomir-фактура is the first, training stage of the project pointing the way towards the achievement of final PROJEKT ATOL goals.

* Communication will be developed through technological, representational (awareness of fiction/non fiction) and pedagogical systems
* Insulation/Isolation autonomy (a new category) will be achieved through energy/material and space/time autonomy and independence. The dematerialisation of logos will be replaced by the logoisation of the material.

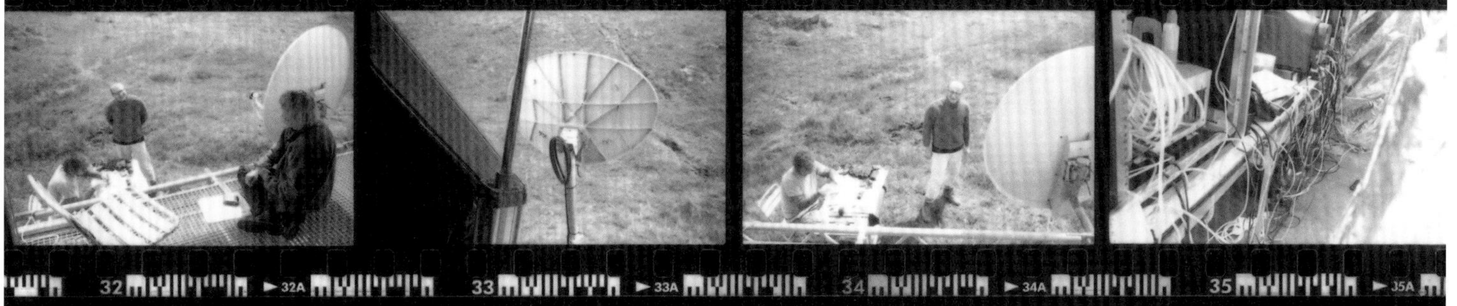

WEATHER AND CLIMATE

TION
CTION
G AND REFLECTION
AND REFLECTION
MIGRATORY PATTERNS
LGORITHMS
PPING AND REFLECTION
DOPPLER NETWORK DEVELOPMENT
G AND REFLECTION
APABILITY ASSESSMENT

- REMOTE SENSING DATA ANALYSIS AND PRESENTATION
- SeaWiFS/TERRA/AQUA PARTNERSHIP
- SENSOR AND REMOTE SENSOR DEVELOPMENT AND DEPLOYMENT
- SEEDS C (SHARED ENVIRONMENTAL EDUCATION DATA SYSTEM on CLIMATE)
- AEROSONDE UAV CONTINUOUS ANTARCTIC OPERATIONS
- ANTARCTIC METEOROLOGICAL PUBLIC ACCESS DATABASE
- AURORAL ACTIVITY MONITORING, MAPPING AND REFLECTION
- LOCAL ECOLOGY AWARENESS INFORMATION SYSTEMS
- CORE (COMPREHENSIVE OBSERVATION and RESEARCH ENVIRONMENT) DEVELOPMENT

CLOSED ENERGY CYCLE DEVELOPMENT
BIOSPHERIC ENVIRONMENT SYSTEMS IMPLEMENTATION
ROBOTIC SENSOR DEPLOYMENT
NON LINEAR AND NON HIERARCHIC DATA DISPLAY AND USAGE
AUTONOMOUS SOCIAL SYSTEM IMPLEMENTATION
AUTONOMOUS ZONE ESTABLISHMENT

2004
- MAKROLAB mark V PROJECT PRESENTATION
- MAKROLAB mark V DEVELOPMENT
- TESTBED SETUP AND STRUCTURAL TESTING: February-May
- SENSOR AND COMM SYSTEMS DETERMINATION: February-May
- SOFTWARE AND HARDWARE REQUIREMENT DETERMINATION: May-October
- ELECTRONICS SYSTEMS INTEGRATION: October-November
- PROTOTYPE PREPRODUCTION ACTIVITIES: November-December
- PUBLIC ARCHIVES PRESENTATION: December
- MAKROLAB mark IIex CONTAINERIZATION AND SHIPPING

2005
- MAKROLAB mark V PROTOTYPE PRODUCTION START: January
- MAKROLAB mark V PROTOTYPE LAUNCH: July
- MAKROLAB mark IIex FIFTH OPERATIONAL SETUP: Southern Africa
- MAKROLAB mark IIex OPERATIONS: August-December
- MAKROLAB TRANSNATIONAL ANTARCTIC FOUNDATION
  ESTABLISHMENT: December, South Pole
- INSULAR TECHNOLOGIES NETWORK 10 NETWORK NODES
  OPERATIONAL: December
- INSULAR TECHNOLOGIES ANTARCTIC TEST: December

2006
- MAKROLAB mark IIex SHIPPING
- MAKROLAB mark IIex SIXTH OPERATIONAL SETUP: Nunavut, Canada
- MAKROLAB mark IIex OPERATIONS: March-June
- MAKROLAB mark IIex DECOMMISSION AND
  FINAL POSITIONING: Nunavut, Canada
- MAKROLAB mark V CONTAINERIZATION AND SHIPPING
- MAKROLAB mark V SEVENTH OPERATIONAL SETUP: Iceland
- MAKROLAB mark V OPERATIONS: July-September
- MAKROLAB TRANSNATIONAL FOUNDATION
  CONFERENCE: Reykyavik, Iceland
- MAKROLAB mark V CONTAINERIZATION AND SHIPPING
- MAKROLAB mark Vex MODIFICATION START

2007
- MAKROLAB Vex MODIFIED SYSTEMS AND MATERIALS TESTING
- MAKROLAB Vex ADVANCED SYSTEMS INTEGRATION AND TESTING
- ANTARCTIC TERRITORIES BASE CAMP EXPEDITION: January
- CONTAINERIZATION, SHIPPING, LOGISTICS
- FLIGHT CAMPAIGN: November, December
- MAKROLAB FOUNDATION TRANSNATIONAL ANTARCTIC
  OPERATIONS START: December

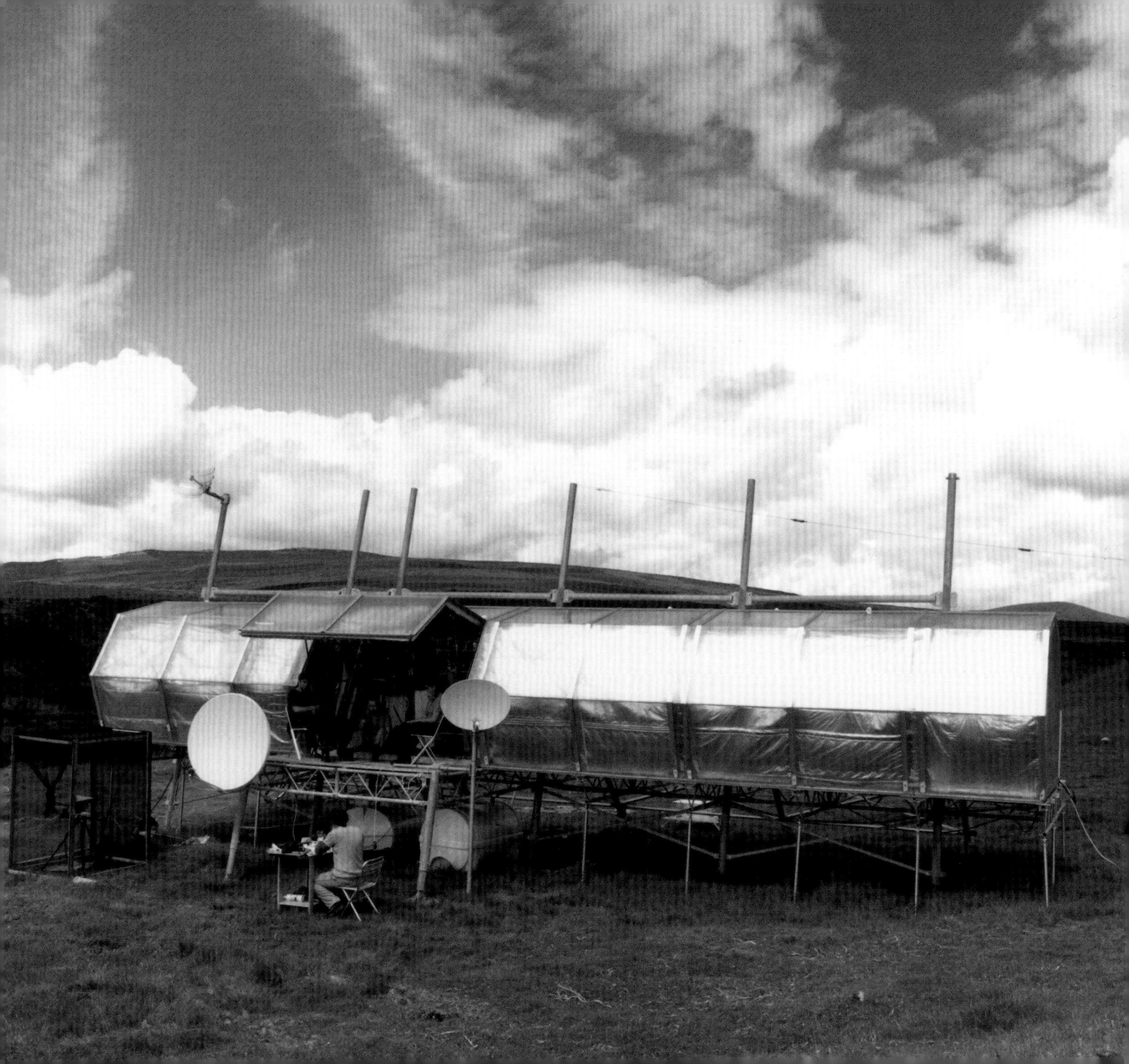

Here's a run down of the last few days:
The power has been going out each night and sometimes during the day at pretty constant intervals. Last night it cut out before Spiderman found out WHO was hurt in the crowd of people past the police line!!!!!! NOOOO!!!! It has been raining on and off for days now and my boots are so drenched they make me feel damp all the way through, even if I am not. Three days ago E. pointed out some wellies in my size. They have completely changed my life as much as the first time I got a real pair of hiking boots. I can go ANYWHERE! Doesn't matter how deep the swamp and it is very deep around the pod.
I remembered my dreams for the first time last night, before I could only recall sensations. They were strange and complicated scenario dreams - overlapping and chaotic. Slept nine hours again last night. It is so nice in here once all tucked in.

We were tired yesterday. E. was really tired. We all took turns taking hot hot baths at the bothy. High luxury straight into the bones.
E. and I visited Glacier Books again. So generous — C. lent me gorgeous early editions of The Farthest North, The Worst Journey in the World and The Icy North

Atholl Estates aerial survey, Landsat images

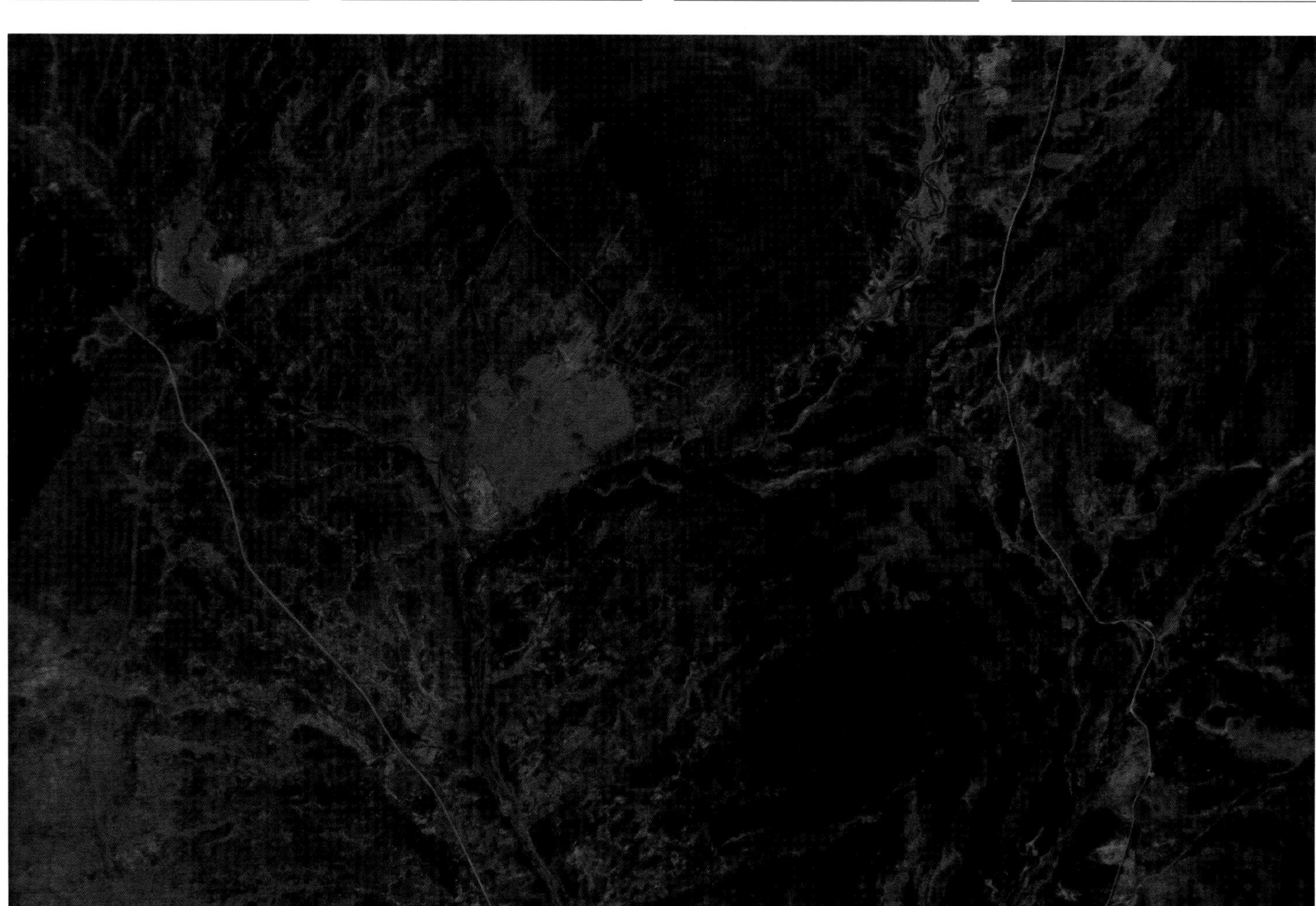

Fritdjof Nansen's description of how and why they decided to work with and not against the drift ice is so beautiful. Began a correspondence with a polar expert in Rhode Island in a search for frozen dreams and crystal libraries.
I didn't know that in addition to writing Arctic Explorations: The Second Grinnell Expedition in Search of Sir John Franklin, Dr. Kane also wrote:The Love Life of Dr.Kane
So high drama! At night we had bedtime stories. I read The Farthest North aloud to T. and E.
E. has become a narcoleptic. (generator off, turbine immobile, for a while no water) If you even mention that the electricity has cut out again he is asleep within minutes, no matter what time of day. The other night when the generator was still down, M. suggested we change its gas canister for the one in the kitchen. T. would have been traumatised had he heard the news, as we have already discussed the

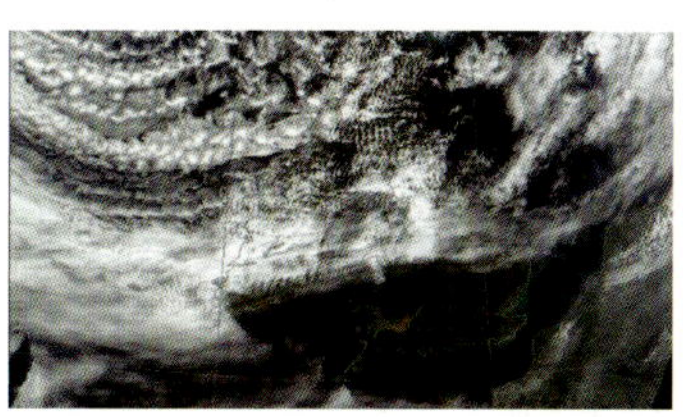

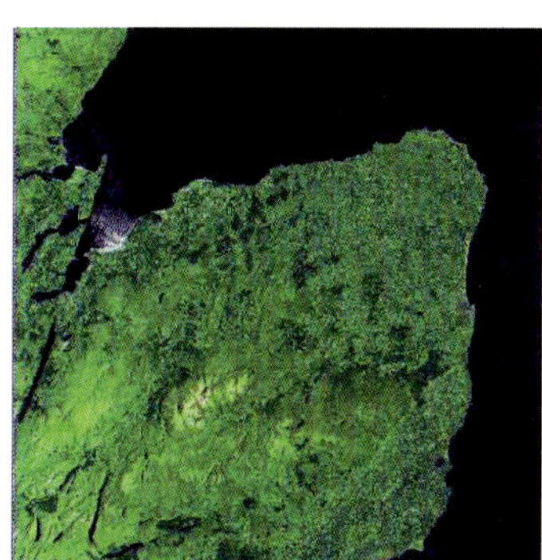

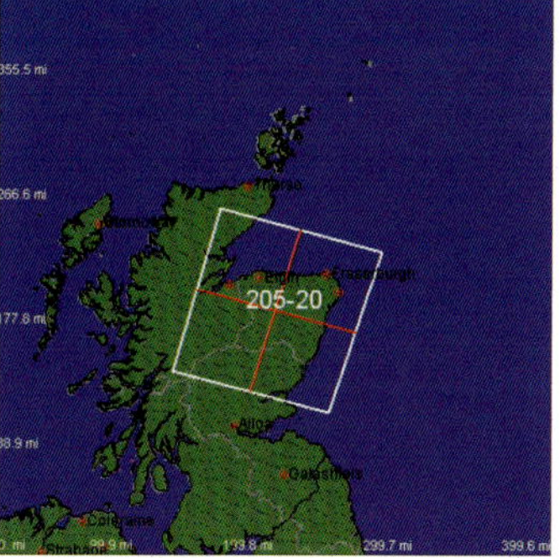

necessity of maintaining the possibility of a hot cup of tea or coffee even if all other technology fails. I will not mention M.'s proposal – I think he will faint. We made the call from the Bothy because we are cold and it is the best place to get a signal. As soon as the call was over I turned my head and found E. already sound asleep on the sofa. Shame. He fixes everything though – maestro. Yesterday was a funny day. The way E. was so tired two days ago is the way I felt yesterday. I woke up wrong. Bumping into stuff, really clumsy – culminating in a grand gesture of dropping the honey bottle into my glass of red wine at dinner and causing a huge mess which, as a Virgo I loathe and detest.

Suddenly, I had a migraine after three hours of trying to do some really basic stuff on line with the speed so slow that it just crashed over and over again. We went to Pitlochry to develop a roll of film and go to the local library. Hundreds of romance novels - no exaggeration, some books on fishing, other stuff. No Don Quixote for E. and no James Hutton for me. No big surprise I guess.

Then to the cafe!

We had:

2 apple tarts with apricot jam on top

54

1
text: Excerpt from An appeal by the Presidents of Planet Earth (Vozzvanie predsedatelej zemnogo šara), translated by Paul Schmidt, edited by Charlotte Douglas from the DIA Art Khlebnikov translation project.

Top right:
photograph: Norman McBeath

Centre:
Anna Jakomulska, Abigail Reynolds, Matthew Biederman
photograph: Fraser MacDonald

3, 5, 7, 9, 11, 13, 15, 17, 19, 21, 23, 25, 27, 29, 31, 35, 37, 39, 41, 43, 51, 53, 55
Top right
EOS TERRA – SeaWiFS satellite MODIS instrument composite images, processed at the Dundee University satellite receiving station, June – July 2002

4
Top left: photograph:
Fraser MacDonald
Top middle: Blair Castle, photograph: Fraser MacDonald
Top right: Marko Peljhan and guest, photograph: Stephen Kovats
Bottom left: photograph:
Fraser MacDonald
Bottom middle: photograph:
Fraser MacDonald
Bottom right: Helen Evans, photograph: Honor Harger

5
Left: photograph: Stephen Kovats
Right: photograph: Paul Khera

8
Left: Tim Knowles and Honor Harger, photograph: Adam Hyde
Right: wind turbine, photograph: Honor Harger

13
photographs: Gavin Starks

16
Painting of The Hermitage
From The tour of Doctor Prosody, in search of the antique and the picturesque by William Combe (London, 1821).

17
Makrolab interior
photograph: Gavin Starks

20
Top left and bottom left: Balloon Drawing Machine, photographs: Tim Knowles
Middle, top right and bottom right: photographs: Honor Harger

21
photograph: Tim Knowles & Gavin Starks

22
photographs: Gavin Starks

24
Adam Hyde builds a 50 miliwatt FM transmitter, and creates FM Radio Makrolab, photographs: Honor Harger

28
photographs: Miles Chalcraft & Dan Belasco Rogers

29
photograph: Katrin Lund

36
ESMI – Open Source Intelligence photographs: PACT Systems archive

37
Ilana Halperin and Tomasz Szymura, photograph: Ewen Chardronnet

41
Left and bottom right:
The Heliographer, photographs: Ewen Chardronnet
Top right: Ewen Chardronnet, photograph: Honor Harger

44
photograph: Norman McBeath

47
photograph: Norman McBeath
text: Velimir Khlebnikov from Tables of Destiny (Otryvok iz dosok sud'by) translated by Paul Schmidt, edited by Charlotte Douglas from the DIA Art Khlebnikov translation project.

48
Mjesec territory, Island of Krk,1994
photograph: Marko Peljhan

51
photograph: Norman McBeath

52, 53
Atholl Estates aerial survey, Landsat images – source material for Anna Jakomulska's project

56
Bottom left: Helena Johard, Ewen Chardronnet, Tom Mulcaire photographs: Gavin Starks

Front cover:
Makrolab, Clunes Beat, Gleann a'Chrombaidh, Atholl Estates, Scotland, 2002
photograph: Tim Knowles

Back cover:
Makrolab interior / exterior photographs: Gavin Starks, www.dgen.net

The Arts Catalyst
Toynbee Studios
28 Commercial Street
London E1 6LS
UK
T +44 (0) 20 7375 3690
F +44 (0) 20 7377 0298
www.artscatalyst.org
info@artscatalyst.org

Zavod Projekt Atol
Ane Ziherlove 2
1000 Ljubljana
Slovenia
T +386-1-5635246
F +386-1-5635247
http://makrolab.ljudmila.org
makrolab@mail.ljudmila.org

http://www.tramway.org

Published by The Arts Catalyst and Zavod Projekt Atol in association with Tramway

Makrolab was created by Marko Peljhan in 1994 and is managed by the Projekt Atol Institute. Makrolab in Scotland was organised by The Arts Catalyst with Projekt Atol Institute, in partnership with Tramway in Glasgow and the Centre for Mountain Studies at Perth College, Scotland.

All rights reserved: no part of this book may be reproduced in any form without the written permission of the publisher.

© 2003 The Arts Catalyst, on behalf of the contributors

Edited by Rob La Frenais, Gillean Dickie and Paul Khera
Designed at PKMB
Printed by Orchid

floating in a sea of light cream, a dollop (awful word) of whipped cream, 2 blueberries, 1/2 of 1 strawberry on each tart, 2 mint leaves and some powdered sugar 1 chocolate cake, 1 mint leaf, chocolate sauce, 1 scoop of vanilla ice cream, 1 strawberry 1 coke 1 mint tea 1 filter coffee, black with sugar

In the morning the lab is very cold. We have decided we should become inchworms in our sleeping bags and crawl along the floor all day.
C. from Glacier books came to the lab today. He brought a copy of Kane's book - dark green with a beautiful detailed gold embossing on the front of a Polar scene with stars. I made

all the boys talk at the other end of the lab while I read sections from the Polar library. I made a hot lunch of Quorn sausages with onion and courgette to be eaten with brown bread and hot mustard. For dinner, E. made whole wheat spaghetti with smoked salmon and yoghurt. Great news – two for one sale on at the

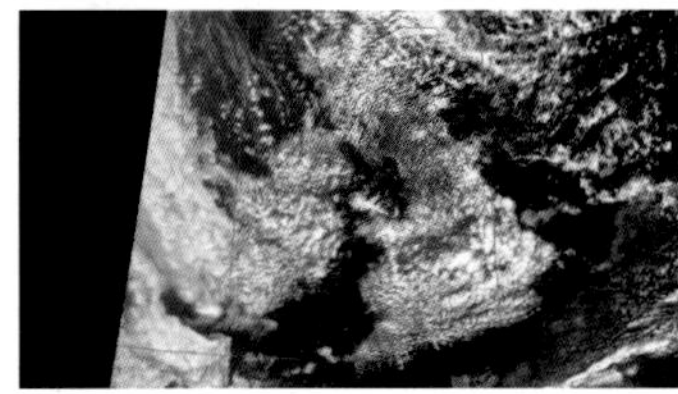

Curating was never so like caretaking. For three months I was ferrying people, objects, supplies, electronic components, wastewater, portable toilets (full), local children and dogs up and down the umbilical track between the lab and the base camp of the Bothy where I also acted as gatekeeper for visitors and press. The role of the curator in an odd way turned full circle, from the keeper of dusty preserved objects in glass cases to (just about) preserved living human microcultures in a tubular habitat. And a sense of peering

in from the outside. One day I arrived at the Makrolab after a 24 hour interval dripping wet from the hill, entering the hydraulic hatch, to find the lab's inhabitants all staring at screens, on beds, at the workstations, a silence punctuated by the odd muffled giggle. Hi everyone, how's it going? no answer. After 5 minutes of being ignored I check the nearest screen. Lines of text - 'Rob just came in, he's dripping wet'. Next line. 'I wonder if he'll make coffee'. There's an animated electronic conversation raging between 6 people a

metre away from each other. The lab had become a hive. Then I realised the hive extends all the way out to people in places like Antarctica, all wondering if I'm going to make coffee. I am tending a node of a global organism. I unloaded the food and made coffee.

Rob La Frenais
Curator of Makrolab
in Scotland

The Centre for Mountain Studies is part of a new academic institution based on the use of modern communications technologies. We were looking for projects to increase awareness of the diverse values of Scotland's mountains during the International Year of Mountains (IYM) 2002, when I was contacted about the Makrolab project. The idea of bringing together artists and scientists in a unique working environment – both indoors and outdoors – utilising new communications technologies and promoting sustainable

practices was the type of innovative project we were looking for.

I was glad to be able to make the connection between Makrolab and the Atholl Estates and to enable scientists interested in mountain environments to hear about the unusual research opportunity of the Makrolab residencies. Makrolab's website and public communications also created new opportunities for communicating the importance of mountains.

Martin Price, Director, Centre for Mountain Studies, Perth College, University of Highlands and Islands

Co-op! Always the bargain hunter even in a remote environment... We were very happy and then we went to sleep. Yesterday we made a most spectacular trip to Glen Tilt on the Atholl Estate – Site of James Hutton's geological revelation regarding contact between magma and country rock. (scandalous contact I might add)
Shook the geology world like a 6.5 on the Richter Scale
We all took turns filming and being intrepid explorers... All the best from the pod, where I am now the only remaining crew member. Don't worry – everyone else has not been swept away by the unexpected gales leaving me to fend for myself among the deer. They have all just gone to Edinburgh.
Ilana Halperin

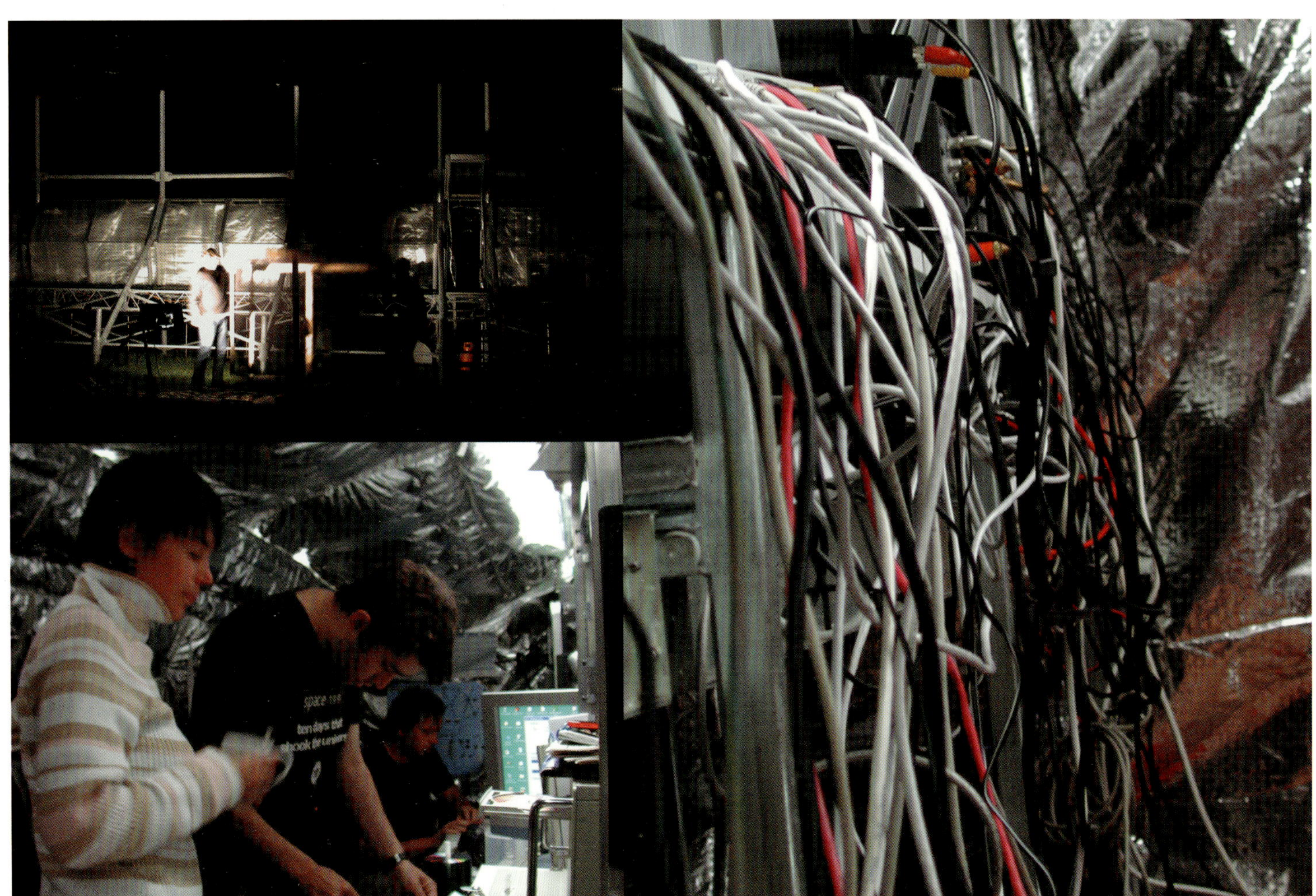